Erwin S. Stanton

Successful
Personnel Recruiting
& Selection

57573

A DIVISION OF AMERICAN MANAGEMENT ASSOCIATIONS

Library of Congress Cataloging in Publication Data
Stanton, Erwin Schoenfeld.
    Successful personnel recruiting & selection.

    Includes index.
    1. Recruiting of employees. 2. Personnel
management. I. Title.
HF5549.5.R44S74   658.31'1   77-21384
ISBN 0-8144-5450-X

© 1977 AMACOM
A division of American Management Associations,
New York.

Fourth Printing

To my wife, Inge,
and my daughters
Suzanne and Nancy
for their support and encouragement

Preface

*I*T IS COMMONLY accepted that management's main job is to get appropriate results through the effective use of people. The first step toward the proper use of an organization's human resources is to hire the right people. The purpose of this book is to offer a tried, proved, and practical system to recruit, interview, and select personnel successfully. These people should then be able to make a useful and worthwhile contribution to the organization that has employed them.

The book is intended for every professional, full-time personnel specialist responsible for providing staff support to other departments throughout his or her organization and who is concerned with developing better ways of recruiting, interviewing, and selecting applicants for a large variety of positions.

In addition, it should be of practical value to operating managers who would like to improve their skills in selecting people, whether they have the services of a professional personnel department available or whether they must handle the staffing function themselves. They may be managers who hire only a limited number of people each year, or their staffing needs may be such that a substantial part of their time is regularly taken up with recruiting and hiring. Examples of such people might include a plant manager about to hire a staff engineer; an office manager who needs to add an accountant; a sales manager recruiting to expand a field sales force; a branch manager of a brokerage firm looking for a securities sales trainee; a director of nursing at a hospital seeking an addition to the nursing staff; and a factory foreman in need of a skilled machine operator. In short, it is hoped that this book will be a useful guide to *any* manager in *any* kind of business or nonprofit organization who wants to be able to select the best possible people to fill the openings in his department.

Selecting personnel is not a new field, and this is certainly not the first book of its kind. Why, then, yet another book on this subject? My answer is that, on the basis of my experience as both a personnel executive and a consulting management psychologist, I feel that there is a need for a new and more systematic approach toward selecting personnel, one that will be more effective and less time consuming than the techniques now practiced by many organizations. Specifically, the book offers a *Sequential Selection System,* which has been designed to enable the interviewer to select very quickly and effectively those applicants most likely to perform successfully. With this technique, an interviewer need not spend time in nonproductive activity.

No book on this subject would be complete if it did not deal concretely with an employer's obligations with respect to equal employment opportunity laws and affirmative action requirements. Even though this particular area is a dynamic one that is constantly undergoing change, it is essential to understand the regulations in their present state and to look ahead to try to anticipate their future direction.

In the very last chapter, we shall put the system to work. You will sit in and observe a simulated employment interview; you will then be asked to make a decision whether to hire the applicant or not. Finally, you will compare your assessment of the applicant with the actual facts.

Recruiting and selecting personnel is really an art and a skill. Like any skill, it can be sharpened. That is the purpose of this book.

No doubt many events, factors, and people have influenced me during the twenty-five years I have worked in the area of human resource utilization. While it is difficult to single out any specific source, I would like to acknowledge the influence of Dr. Robert N. McMurry, one of the nation's pioneering industrial psychologists, who has made very substantial contributions to the field of personnel selection.

Erwin S. Stanton, Ph.D.

Contents

one

Introduction and preview

"$\mathcal{P}$EOPLE ARE our most important asset." This statement has been made so often and by so many companies over the course of years that it has become trite and overworked. Nevertheless, it is more significant than ever, particularly as many organizations have seen their labor costs rise dramatically. A company's personnel is, indeed, a valuable asset. In fact, it may very well be the organization's prime asset.

The quality of a company's personnel is frequently the single factor that determines whether the organization is going to be successful, whether it will realize a satisfactory return on its investment, and whether it will reach its basic objectives. Indeed, if proper personnel selection was vital during the years when the United States was predominantly a production-oriented economy, it is even more important now that the major part of our nation's gross national product has its source in rendering services.

Much has been written on how to train and develop employees effectively as well as on various ways to motivate them so that they will be able to make a truly worthwhile contribution to the company. These management activities are unquestionably important, and no company can afford to ignore them. However, if the wrong employee has been selected initially, no training program or motivational system—no matter how well conceived and designed—is likely to compensate adequately or offset the original error made in hiring such a person.

The tremendous cost of such training makes it all the more critical that a great deal of careful attention be focused on the initial selection of a company's labor force to ensure that such training efforts will fall on fertile soil. And since so many higher echelon jobs are filled by employees already within the organization, proper scrutiny must be given to the initial selection process to make certain that a sufficient number of promotable candidates are constantly brought into the organization. Also, they will have to be replaced as they qualify for more responsible positions and rise within the company.

THE COST OF POOR
PERSONNEL SELECTION

In recent years, the cost of hiring employees has risen substantially. Although all companies realize that it has become quite expensive, few have actually calculated the costs precisely. Companies that have researched the question have reported figures ranging anywhere from a low of $300 for a factory applicant to an amount well into five figures for a middle to higher level executive or professional employee. The median figure currently estimated is in the vicinity of $1,750. This amount is usually thought to cover such components as the cost of newspaper advertising, employment agency fees, interviewing time, and administrative costs.

Several years ago, I was asked to review the college recruiting program of a Fortune 100 company that was hiring approximately 3,000 to 4,000 graduates from the nation's campuses each year. The company estimated that, on the basis of some 3,500 graduates hired annually, maintaining its college recruiting program cost an average of $1,000 for each graduate hired. Nor do the costs end, of course, with the placement of the new employee on the job, for that person obviously will require a certain degree of training—either formally or on the job. And many times the cost of training surpasses hiring costs. A good case in point is the expense involved in training a securities sales representative for Wall Street. The requirements of the New York Stock Exchange call for a newly hired trainee to spend four months learning the brokerage business before he can be admitted to take the New York Stock Exchange examination that qualifies him to begin trading on behalf of a customer. One leading brokerage firm estimates that it costs the company $18,000 to train each broker candidate in the essentials of the securities business before he will make his very first trade.

Obviously, the cost of improper selection of personnel can be very high. When the unsuccessful employee must be terminated, the recruiting and interviewing process must begin all over again, and the successor must first be trained before being put on the job. These costs, however, are only the more visible ones. The hidden costs are frequently even higher: low quality of work performed by the unsuccessful employee while still on the job; the internal disorganization and disruption that employee may have caused; the customer ill will and alienation that may have been generated; and perhaps even the actual loss of a much valued account.

MARGINAL EMPLOYEES

More often than not, the really unsatisfactory job applicant is screened out as part of the traditional employment process and does not get onto the payroll. Those who somehow "slip through" usually reveal their deficiencies and shortcomings early and are soon terminated. This is not the case, however, with the "marginal" or borderline employee. Regrettably, virtually all organizations have some marginal employees on their payroll. In retrospect these people probably should never have been hired in the first place. Nevertheless, in many instances they have been with the company longer than management would care to acknowledge.

What do I mean by the "marginal" employee? Simply stated, I would define him as someone who really is not capable enough to be considered truly satisfactory; one who has failed to make a worthwhile contribution to the company. Neither, however, is he so grossly incompetent or ineffectual that he must be discharged immediately. The problem is that too many companies employ too many marginal employees. Once they are on the payroll, it frequently becomes exceedingly difficult to fire them—especially with the passing of time. When they were first hired, their deficiencies and shortcomings may not have been readily apparent; after all, they are usually on their very best behavior during the interview. Not until they are on the job for a while do their limitations become visible.

Frequently marginal employees are hired by the company when it is in the midst of an expansion program; under the pressure of the moment, they are not properly screened out. Often the interviewer realizes that the particular applicant does not really meet all the critical requirements for the position in question. However, there may be a certain degree of pressure to fill the position; the job may have been open for an excessively long time; and the personnel specialist may have received several not-so-gentle reminders that the vacancy is still unfilled. Under these circumstances, it is only human for the interviewer to rationalize recommending such a person, reasoning that "If you can't get what you want, you must take what you can get." To defend his action, he is very likely to express the sincere but usually fruitless hope that with time and training the applicant will develop into a better employee than he appears to be.

In reality, this hope is rarely fulfilled. If anything, the marginal applicant usually turns out to be even less satisfactory an employee than expected, and becomes a millstone around his department's neck. Because he lacks basic motivation and attitudinal qualifications, he will never really be capable of earning his keep. By definition, he is not promotable and will never be able to grow with the company.

A particular case will clearly illustrate the dilemma facing the company that has hired an excessive number of marginal or borderline applicants. Several years ago, my firm was called in to make a psychological evaluation of the qualifications of a company's national sales force. The assignment was prompted by the president's dissatisfaction with the performance of the organization's sales representatives. Indeed, this company was referred to as the "sleeping giant" of the industry. While the company's competition was chalking up a high sales volume, its sales production was clearly in the doldrums.

A detailed analysis of the company's typical sales representative revealed the profile of a very likable and well-meaning person, but one who clearly lacked ambition, drive, and initiative and simply was not interested in working very hard. In short, most of these salesmen were basically marginal employees who should never have been hired in the first place. Unfortunately, by now they had been with the company a long time, without ever contributing very much to its growth and progress.

Clearly, time and training could not overcome the basic deficiency of these salesmen. In retrospect, they should never have been permitted to join the sales force. Once on the job, since they were holding down a sales territory and at least showing the corporate flag and writing some business, they were tolerated and kept on the payroll. But they were never really successful, and failed completely to generate a satisfactory volume of business for the company.

In the course of the traditional personnel staffing process, a certain number of marginal candidates will apply for employment. There is always the risk that some of them will be hired if the interviewer is not careful and astute enough to detect the areas of marginality. I believe that the selection system that will be introduced later in this book can help the personnel specialist to discover the significant areas of marginality in an applicant *before* he is hired, enabling the specialist to reject such a candidate.

WHY GOOD PEOPLE
ARE ALWAYS HARD TO FIND

Most companies have long recognized that the success of their organizations depends greatly on the quality and competence of their personnel. Indeed, research documents that of all the variables that contribute to the success and viability of an organization, none is more important than the quality of the people involved. Therefore, it is not at all surprising that companies are so eager to attract, hire, and retain a productive, satisfied, and well-motivated staff.

It is a truism that well-qualified and competent people are always hard to find. Even when the economy is soft, as for example during a recession, truly good people are hard to come by. Consequently, they must be aggressively and imaginatively sought out and recruited. Operating managers sometimes find it hard to believe that the personnel department is encountering difficulty in filling a particular job, especially when newspapers and the TV media report high rates of unemployment. However, in recent years the labor market has frequently seen a variety of paradoxes. For example, unemployed aeronautical engineers may be looking for work in the greater Los Angeles area, but these people cannot be hired as programmers or accountants, although the latter are in critically short supply in most parts of the country. The Detroit automobile assembly worker who is laid off as a result of falling sales of new cars cannot be transferred to fill an opening for a console operator in the company's electronic data processing department.

There are many reasons good people are traditionally hard to find. With some exceptions, the years since World War II have seen a tremendous growth in the nation's economy. Few organizations have not vigorously and even dramatically expanded. Companies have moved into new product and service areas, they have expanded geographically into other parts of the country, and the trend toward decentralization of operations has brought about the need for additional personnel. The nonprofit and institutional sector also—particularly government service, health care institutions, and schools and colleges—has grown and expanded significantly.

However, with increased emphasis on well-trained specialists in virtually every area, all organizations have found themselves in competition with other organizations for available competent personnel—people Peter Drucker has referred to as the "knowledge workers." In many critical occupations and professions, companies have seen the demand for quality applicants go up as the supply went down. For this reason, if a company is going to be successful in attracting well-qualified job applicants, it must maintain an aggressive, imaginative, and well-designed recruiting program.

THE SEQUENTIAL SELECTION SYSTEM

Effective staffing and success in recruiting and selecting truly capable people who will be an asset to the organization require a certain amount of time, effort, and careful attention in the employment process. All too often personnel specialists—as well as operating managers, who frequently handle the entire selection process themselves because their organizations do not maintain a separate personnel department—spend an inordinate amount of time without accomplishing very much. Too much time is spent on lengthy interviews with job applicants who are not qualified and who should be promptly, albeit tactfully and gracefully, screened out. In other words, sometimes personnel specialists or operating managers work "hard," but not "smart," spinning their wheels unproductively. That is why I developed a more streamlined staffing system several years ago. Its purpose is to recruit and select competent personnel promptly and competently, without wasting time on unqualified applicants.

Steps in the Sequential Selection System

Subsequent chapters will detail each of the vital steps that should be followed chronologically in installing the Sequential Selection System. First, let us take a quick look at each specific step in the system.

Step 1: Determining Accurate and Realistic Staffing Specifications

Before the recruiting, interviewing, and selecting process can even begin, we must obtain a precise description of the particular job we want to fill and get a very clear idea of all the relevant aspects of the assignment essential to our complete knowledge and understanding of the position. After this very important step, we will be ready to determine the exact qualifications needed by the job applicant.

Step 2: Effective Applicant Recruiting

To a considerable extent, the success we have in selecting really good employees is a direct function of the quality and quantity of the applicants we have been able to attract and to recruit. It is obvious that only people who have expressed interest in joining our company—in essence, those who have applied—can eventually be considered for employment. If we are to have any type of truly selective employment system, we must have a sufficient number of well-qualified applicants to choose from. Step 2 will focus on the importance of an aggressive, imaginative, and continuous recruiting program and will take a close look at some of the more useful recruiting sources that might be utilized.

Step 3: Initial Applicant Screening

Having succeeded in recruiting a satisfactory number of well-qualified job applicants, our next step is to screen out those who, for one reason or another, are clearly not suited for the position. Here I draw a very definite distinction between *initial* applicant screening and the more detailed and in-depth selection interview that, according to my system, will take place at a later stage. In this third sequential step, we will focus on specific ways unqualified applicants can be screened out without wasting too much time on them.

Step 4: Checking the Applicant's Employment References

Applicants who have successfully passed the initial screening stage should now have their employment references checked. My discussion of this topic will focus on the importance of conducting a thorough reference check of all the applicant's former employers. I will explore the various ways to obtain employment references—in person, by mail, and by telephone. I prefer the telephone reference check, and I will discuss why.

Step 5: The Structured Selection Interview

Following the strategy outlined previously in the Sequential Selection System, the less qualified job applicants have by now been expeditiously rejected as a result of initial screening and perhaps skill and ability tests and the telephone reference check. Candidates who have successfully survived these preliminary hurdles are then given a thorough selection interview, which will be the focus of a later chapter.

Step 6: Evaluating the Applicant and Arriving at a Decision

Having obtained all the necessary and pertinent facts regarding the qualifications of the job applicant, we are now ready to arrive at a final decision—whether or not to hire him. In this step, I will offer a conceptual model. The interviewer will be able to use it to list and analyze the applicant's key strengths and assets as well as his major limitations, weaknesses, and developmental needs. Next, his strengths and weaknesses will be matched against the specific requirements of the particular job for which he is being considered to see how close a fit there is between the ideal candidate and the actual job applicant. We shall obtain both a numerical and a descriptive rating that will indicate the overall suitability of the applicant and permit us to make a definite decision to employ or reject him.

Advantages of the Sequential Selection System

The Sequential Selection System has achieved excellent results for many organizations all over the country. The reasons for its practical usefulness are many:

1. *It saves a great deal of time.* The system basically streamlines the entire staffing process by minimizing the amount of wasted time. Applicants who are not qualified are speedily rejected, thus freeing the personnel specialist to engage in more useful and productive activity.

2. *It improves the prediction of probable future job success.* As a result of the system, both the personnel specialist and the operating manager will find that their

ability to predict the applicant's future on-the-job performance will improve substantially.

3. *Personnel turnover is significantly reduced.* Through better selection, fewer marginal or unsatisfactory applicants will be hired, and a larger number of potentially successful candidates will be brought into the organization.

4. *Personnel staffing becomes a smoothly operating function.* The Sequential Selection System is designed to facilitate the entire staffing process so as to minimize the incidence of acrimony or discord that so often accompanies other employment systems or strategies. Perhaps most important is the fact that the system is well accepted by job applicants, who feel that in every instance they have been given fair and complete consideration of their application for employment.

5. *The system is completely compatible with all equal employment opportunity and affirmative action requirements.* By following the system, a company's entire staffing program will be completely in keeping with all current government requirements with respect to the vital area of equal employment opportunity.

Before we embark on a comprehensive and detailed study of the Sequential Selection System, we must understand fully all the key government requirements and regulations as they apply to the field of equal employment opportunity and affirmative action compliance. Indeed, it has become crystal clear in recent years that virtually whatever we do in the employment process is in one way or another subject to a variety of federal laws, government guidelines, and court interpretative decisions. This vital area will be covered in the next chapter.

two

A guide to equal employment opportunity requirements

RECRUITING AND selecting people for employment has become much more complex in recent years. And it is likely to become more complex, involved, and difficult in the

Author's Note: The information in this chapter is intended for management training and development purposes only. The information presented has been carefully researched from government publications, federal laws, and court decisions and rulings. The contents should not be construed, however, as a final and definitive legal document. If more specific legal assistance is required, appropriate professional resources should be sought. Adapted from Erwin S. Stanton, "The Manager's Guide to Equal Employment Opportunity Requirements," 2nd edition, E. S. Stanton & Associates, Inc., New York, 1977.

foreseeable future. Beginning in the early and middle 1960s and continuing to gather momentum are vast social and political changes in our country. These changes have had a dramatic impact on the management and operation of all organizations—both profitmaking and nonprofitmaking.

Of particular significance has been the emergence of a vast array of laws, government regulations, federal guidelines, court decisions, and interpretive rulings affecting the employment and utilization of minority personnel and women. There is today no doubt whatsoever that *equal employment opportunity for all persons irrespective of race, color, religion, ethnic origin, sex, or age has firmly become the law of the land.* The law is enforced ever more vigorously, with substantial financial penalties being imposed on organizations who do not comply completely with current requirements. As many employers have learned—and at considerable cost—the laws are tough, and intelligent, capable, and zealous regulatory administrators are determined to remedy actively what they believe to be the results of years of prior discriminatory practices.

As a result, both personnel practitioners and managers at every level must be thoroughly informed on present equal employment opportunity requirements if they are to satisfy all the current regulations and avoid—or at least minimize—costly and time-consuming encounters with federal, state, and local government regulatory bodies. The purpose of this chapter is to acquaint you with current equal employment opportunity requirements and to indicate what, under present regulations, you may and may not do.

The information offered in this chapter is intended to serve as a practical, concise, and useful guide. However, it is *not* meant to be the definitive and final legal word in the area of equal employment opportunity compliance. Nor am I suggesting that following these guidelines will grant an organization permanent immunity from any future charges alleging discriminatory practices. No guide could ever make such a claim in view of the dynamic and ever-changing nature of the field. Indeed, every manager and personnel professional needs to keep himself constantly up to date with respect to regulations and requirements as they evolve. However, I feel that the direction in which federal, state, and local equal employment opportunity requirements are heading is outlined fairly clearly by now. Consequently, by following the suggestions offered in this chapter, you should succeed in meeting the essential goal of full compliance with existing requirements.

WHAT THE LAWS REQUIRE

For a number of years, there was considerable confusion, misunderstanding, and ambiguity with regard to the meaning, interpretation, and application of these various regulations. While there is still a good deal of uncertainty on several key issues that await final clarification in the courts, the entire equal employment opportunity area is much clearer than ever before, with future trends and direction fairly definitively spelled out for management's guidance.

What, then, do the laws require? In general, it is illegal to discriminate on the basis of race, color, religion, sex, age, or national origin in all employment practices, which include hiring, discharging, promotion, compensation, and all other terms, privileges, and conditions of employment. Let us take a closer look at some of the key laws and executive orders that spell out an employer's responsibilities and obligations.

The Equal Employment Opportunity Act of 1972, Including Title VII of the Civil Rights Act of 1964

For most organizations, this is *the* basic law that regulates employment. The Act fundamentally covers employment and all other related aspects irrespective of race, color, religion, sex, or national origin and applies to the following organizations:

All private employers of 15 or more persons
All educational institutions, both public and private
State and local governments
Public and private employment agencies
Labor unions with 15 or more members
Joint labor–management committees for apprenticeship
and training

Under this act, the Equal Employment Opportunity Commission (EEOC) was established to receive and, on its own initiative, to investigate job discrimination complaints and, where the Commission finds the charge to be justified, to attempt through conciliation to reach an agreement. Should it fail in its efforts, however, the Commission has the power to go directly into federal court to enforce the law. In addition, interested organizations may file class action suits on behalf of individuals who feel that they have been discriminated against by their employers. In this connection, these individuals can claim back pay, damages, and legal fees. An aggrieved person can also go into court directly to sue an employer for alleged discriminatory practices. The Equal Employment Opportunity Commission and, more recently, several other federal executive agencies issue appropriate periodic guidelines to assist companies in making sure that their employment systems are in compliance with the law.

Executive Orders Number 11246 and 11375 and Revised Orders Number 4 and 14

These are Presidential Orders rather than laws and affect all organizations that hold government contracts. Adherence to these Executive Orders is administered by the Office of Federal Contract Compliance Programs of the U.S. Department of Labor. The orders apply specifically to contractors and subcontractors who have government contracts in excess of $50,000 or who employ 50 or more people. The orders prohibit discrimination in employment, but also require each organization to develop and implement an *Affirmative Action Program*—which is regularly audited by an assigned federal compliance agency—to remedy the effects of past discriminatory practices and to ensure increased opportunity at all levels for minorities and women.

Specifically, under these Presidential Orders, a government contractor is required to furnish a results-oriented written commitment for an *affirmative action program,* together with specific *goals and timetables* for their attainment. Most significantly, an organization found not to be in compliance with Revised Order Number 4 (which calls for a concrete affirmative action program) faces the possibility of cancellation of its government contracts.

The Equal Pay Act of 1963

This act requires all employers to provide equal pay for *both* men and women *performing similar work* and is administered by the Wage and Hour Division of the U.S. Department of Labor. As a result of several well-publicized court cases, a number of employers (notably the American Telephone & Telegraph Company) have been compelled to make substantial back pay awards to women who have been discriminated against in violation of this act as well as of the Equal Employment Opportunity Act of 1972 and Title VII of the Civil Rights Act of 1964.

The Age Discrimination in Employment Act of 1967

This act, also administered by the Wage and Hour Division of the U.S. Department of Labor, prohibits discrimination in employment against persons between the ages of 40 and 65.*

*As of the summer of 1977, Congress is considering raising the limit to 70.

The Rehabilitation Act of 1973

Section 503 of the Rehabilitation Act of 1973 requires all companies holding federal contracts of $50,000 or more and having 50 or more employees to take affirmative action to employ and advance qualified handicapped individuals who meet reasonable standards for employment that are job related and consistent with business necessity and the safe performance of the job. As part of a company's affirmative action program, reasonable accommodation must be made to the physical and mental limitations of an employee or applicant, unless it can be demonstrated that such an accommodation would impose an undue hardship on the conduct of the company's business.

The Vietnam Era Veterans' Readjustment Assistance Act of 1974

Section 402 of this act requires all organizations holding a government contract in excess of $10,000 to take affirmative action to employ and advance in employment qualified disabled veterans generally and veterans from the Vietnam era, disabled or nondisabled, specifically. The Act further requires contractors to list all their job openings with the appropriate local state employment service.

INTERPRETATIONS, DECISIONS, AND RULINGS BY THE FEDERAL COURTS

The major thrust, however, in the enforcement of equal employment opportunity regulations has not come as a result of the activities of the various federal regulatory agencies. Rather, it has been a direct consequence of a variety of highly significant federal court interpretations and decisions—many of which have resulted in considerable cost to employers through substantial payments for back pay and damages awarded to plaintiffs who have successfully prosecuted their cases. Let us examine precisely how the federal courts have interpreted and given administrative meaning to the various equal employment opportunity requirements.

The stand that the courts have steadfastly taken, and no doubt will continue to take in the future, is that by law, *all the various groups in the labor force are entitled to equal employment opportunity throughout all levels and subdivisions of the organization, unless business necessity precludes such consideration. And the burden of proof rests clearly upon the employer to justify any exception to the general rule of nondiscrimination.*

Furthermore, the courts' interpretations are very broad, pervasive, and comprehensive, and apply basically to any and all facets of the employment process. Included here are such aspects as:

Job specifications
Recruiting sources used to attract job applicants
Screening and interviewing of job applicants
Use of psychological tests
Training and development programs
Promotion, demotion, layoff, and discharge policies
Employee compensation and benefit programs

Specifically, the courts are saying in the broadest possible terms that nondiscrimination in employment is the law. And most significantly, rising out of the landmark Supreme Court decision in *Griggs* v. *Duke Power Company* (401 U.S. 424-1971), the courts have ruled that it is the *results* and the *consequences* of an employer's action—and clearly not his intent, honest and sincere as it may be, not to discriminate—that determine whether he, in fact, is discriminating and thus in line for positive remedial action to remove the effects of past discriminatory practices.

Citing the historic *Griggs* v. *Duke Power Company* case, the courts have ruled that any employment practice or policy, however neutral in intent and however fairly and impartially administered, which has a "disparate effect" (i.e., an uneven or numerically disproportionate impact) on members of a "protected class," as specified in the law, or which perpetuates the effect of previous discriminatory practices, constitutes unlawful discrimination, unless it can be proved that such a policy is absolutely essential because of "business necessity." In that case, it is the responsibility of the employer to substantiate beyond any reasonable doubt that such a policy is necessary for the safe and efficient operation of the business or that a deviation from such a policy is apt to have an extremely adverse financial impact on the company.

It should be noted that in rendering their decisions, the federal courts have been strongly influenced by a company's employment statistics. Specifically, *highly disproportionate representation of minorities or women (or men)* in *any* job category or classification in relation to their presence in the geographic population or work force has been interpreted by the courts to constitute strong evidence of discriminatory practices. Consequently, where such disproportionate representation is found to exist, the courts strongly suspect that somewhere in the organization's employment system, discriminatory practices are prevalent. Again, citing the U.S. Supreme Court decision, "What is required . . . is the removal of artificial, arbitrary and unnecessary barriers to employment when the barriers operate invidiously to discriminate on the basis of racial or other impermissible classification."

In providing concrete guidance for employers, the courts have further ruled that, where barriers to equal employment opportunity exist, positive and *affirmative action* is required by all organizations, *regardless of whether they hold a government contract or not,* to develop new policies and practices that provide all persons equal opportunity for employment. Accordingly, an employer must correct and avoid carrying forward unnecessary adverse impacts resulting from past discrimination. Organizations must establish concrete numerical goals and timetables that will ". . . remove vestiges of past discrimination . . . eliminate present and assure the non-existence of future barriers to (the) full enjoyment of equal job opportunities." Such steps call for seeking out and employing qualified members of all protected groups that are represented in the labor force for opportunities in all parts and at all levels of the organization where they are underrepresented or underutilized.

HOW TO DEVELOP
AN EQUAL EMPLOYMENT OPPORTUNITY
AFFIRMATIVE ACTION PROGRAM

In the previous pages, we have explored what the various equal employment opportunity laws require and how the federal courts are interpreting these laws, noting the financial penalties that have been imposed on numerous companies that have been found in violation of these laws. Let us focus on the specific steps an organization must take to make certain that it is in full compliance with all equal employment opportunity regulations and how it can best develop and implement the required affirmative action program.

Step #1. Issue a Written Equal Employment Opportunity and Affirmative Action Program Policy Statement

In this initial step, top management—preferably the chief executive officer of the company—should issue a written equal employment opportunity and affirmative action commitment. Unless this is done and top management actively supports such a program, it is unlikely that concrete steps will be taken to bring the organization's employment policies into compliance with required regulations.

Top management should issue a firm and definite policy statement that equal employment opportunity for all persons regardless of race, creed, color, sex, national origin, or age is a basic and fundamental company policy, and *that it shall be vigorously enforced.* Furthermore, such a statement should clearly indicate that it calls for an affirmative action program with specific *goals* and *timetables.* Perhaps most important, it should state that all executives, managers, and supervisors will be held accountable for appropriate results and that they will be evaluated on the basis of these results as well as the usual criteria. An excellent example of such a policy commitment is the following message, which was sent to every manager in the company by Peter McColough, chairman of the board of Xerox Corporation:

> I am not satisfied with our progress in the placement of minorities and women in upper level and managerial positions. . . . Achieving these objectives is as important as meeting any other traditional business responsibility. It follows, of course, that a key element in each manager's overall performance appraisal will be his progress in this important area. No manager should expect a satisfactory appraisal if he meets other objectives but fails here.

Here is another example of an effective policy statement:

> The Apex Manufacturing Company is an equal opportunity employer offering employment solely on the basis of ability, qualifications, merit, and physical capability to all persons without discrimination because of race, color, religion, sex, age, or national origin. The goal of our company is to increase the level of employment of minority and female personnel to include professional, managerial, and supervisory positions consistent, however, with the

maintenance of professional performance standards.

Step #2. Appoint a Top Official to Direct and Implement the Program

A top executive should be appointed with the responsibility and authority to direct and implement the company's equal employment opportunity and affirmative action program. This person should have sufficient executive stature and visibility within the organization to command the respect and authority needed to launch the program successfully. Preferably, he should report directly to the chief executive officer. The major functions of this executive should include the following:

1. To keep abreast of the latest legal developments in the area of equal employment opportunity and affirmative action compliance.
2. To disseminate current information to all concerned parties within the organization.
3. To maintain liaison between the company and the various government regulatory bodies as well as with minority and women's organizations and community and other appropriate groups.
4. To coordinate all equal employment opportunity and affirmative action programs throughout the organization.
5. To maintain appropriate records and to prepare the reports that are required periodically by government agencies.

Step #3. Publicize the Company's Program

It is imperative that widespread coverage and publicity be given to the company's program—both internally and outside the organization. *Internally*, this should include such steps as:

- A written communication from the chief executive of the organization stating the company's commitment to the principle of equal employment opportunity.
- A description of the program in the organization's various publications, such as operating manuals, employee handbooks, and house organs.
- Special meetings with executives, managers, supervisors, employees, and union representatives informing them of the organization's commitment to equal employment opportunity.
- Extensive publicity through such means as newsletters, publications, payroll inserts, and bulletin boards.
- Meetings with minority groups and women personnel requesting their active assistance in the implementation of the program.
- Development of appropriate sensitivity and awareness training programs for designated personnel.

Externally, the program should be publicized in the following ways:

- Personal visits as well as written communications informing the company's current and potential recruiting sources of its program.
- Contact with the organization's vendors, suppliers, and contractors.
- Establishment of contact with appropriate outreach recruiting sources that specialize in the placement of minority personnel and women applicants.
- Advertisement of the company's job openings in the minority community media, such as specialized newspapers, magazines, and radio stations.
- Organization of tours through the company's facilities for appropriate minority and women's groups.
- In all newspaper advertising, inclusion of the statement "An Equal Opportunity–Affirmative Action Employer—M/F."

Step #4. Survey the Company's Present Minority and Female (or Male) Employment by Department and Job Classification (Work Force Utilization Analysis)

This step essentially marks the actual launching of a company's equal employment opportunity and affirmative action program. If it is to be successful, it will require the full cooperation of every executive, manager, and supervisor at every level in the organization. At this point both the number and the percentage of minority and female (or male) personnel currently employed in each department and in each major job classification throughout the organization need to be determined. After analysis of the results, the personnel specialist can identify the possible existence of what government compliance agencies refer to as an "underutilization" or a "concentration" of minority personnel and/or females or males.

Underutilization is defined by the government as having a smaller number of minority and/or women (or male) employees in a given job category than would reasonably be expected in the relevant local labor market. For example, very few, or no, women may be employed in a supervisory or managerial capacity.

Concentration means the presence in the organization of a larger number of a particular group in a specific job category or department than would reasonably be expected in the local work force. An illustration would be a predominance of black or Spanish-surnamed personnel in relatively menial or low-level positions.

It is vital to point out that when a federal compliance agency finds *significant disproportionate statistics* in an organization's work force, suggesting the underutilization or concentration of minority or women personnel in the "relevant labor market," the implication usually drawn is that there is a strong probability that some discriminatory practices are currently operating within its employment system calling for positive corrective action.

The "relevant labor market" in a particular geographic area is generally construed by the government to correspond to the Standard Metropolitan Statistical Area (SMSA), data for which can be obtained from the Census Bureau of the U.S. Department of Labor; the Bureau of Labor Statistics, U.S. Department of Labor; and various offices of the state employment service.

Step #5. Develop Specific Affirmative Action Goals and Timetables

Having determined the extent of underutilization or concentration of minority personnel or women in the company, the personnel professional is ready to set specific *numerical goals and timetables* for each department and job classification to remedy the identified imbalance. This step must take into account the dynamic and often unique nature of each organization. Some industries and organizations are constantly changing and growing. Others tend to be more stable and do not have major changes occurring with the same frequency. Consequently, each company will need to develop *near-term, intermediate,* and *long-term* goals and timetables, reflecting the conditions and circumstances of its own organization. Generally speaking, however, it is strongly suggested that to satisfy government requirements, a definite commitment should be made to goals and timetables on at least an annual basis.

Step #6. Develop and Implement the Program

This is the key stage in the entire program and requires a thorough review of the total employment system to identify possible barriers to equal employment opportunity in the organization. Specific aspects of the employment system that need to be analyzed carefully should include:

- All recruitment procedures and referral sources.
- The entire selection process: including job require-

ments, job descriptions, job specifications, preemployment inquiries, application forms, psychological testing, and the selection interview.

- The upward mobility system: including job progression, transfers, seniority provisions, promotion, and training programs.
- Compensation system.
- Benefits, privileges, and conditions of employment.
- Layoff, recall, termination, demotion, discharge, and disciplinary actions.
- Union contract provisions affecting the above procedures.

It is impossible within the framework of this chapter to provide a complete and all-inclusive list of each and every current federal and local equal employment opportunity requirement, because of the constantly changing and dynamic nature of the field. However, the most important and critical aspects that confront the manager and the personnel expert will be discussed in the following sections.

Job Specifications

Many organizations inadvertently violate equal employment opportunity regulations because, *completely unintentionally and unknowingly,* they require *excessive* and *unnecessary* qualifications on the part of prospective job applicants. These often have the effect of rejecting a disproportionate number of individuals protected under the laws. Several key court decisions—in particular the already oft-cited *Griggs* v. *Duke Power Company* case—have consistently upheld the "Guidelines on Employee Selection Procedures" published by the Equal Employment Opportunity Commission. These guidelines fundamentally require an organization's job specifications to meet two basic standards:

1. They must be significantly related to successful job performance.

2. There must be an overriding business necessity requiring the applicant to meet the stated job specifications.

Job relatedness. It is vital, therefore, that every job be critically analyzed to determine that all job specifications are *realistic* and directly *job related.* Very often in the past, employers insisted on excessive, unnecessary, or unrelated qualifications, which had the result of a disproportionately higher rejection rate of minority and women applicants, in violation of the law. Among the most flagrant illegal practices in this context have been:

1. Excessive or unnecessarily high educational requirements, such as the mandatory possession of a high school diploma or college degree.
2. Artificially high prior experience requirements.
3. Insistence that each person hired for a given position have the capacity for early promotion, even if promotion is not likely in the foreseeable future.
4. Physical requirements (such as height or weight) or appearance and dress standards unrelated to successful job performance.

Business necessity. In those rare instances in which an organization specifies a man or woman or a particular age range for a given position, it *must* be ready to defend its requirement and be able to substantiate that the requirement is *essential,* and that business necessity compels it. However, legally, almost all jobs must be open to both men and women. Nor can a company state a preference based on age. Nevertheless, in rare instances an employer may obtain a "bona fide occupational qualification" (BFOQ); for example, in selecting an actor or an actress for a particular role. Still, the courts have interpreted "business necessity" very narrowly, requiring overriding evidence that the discriminatory practice in question is truly essential to the "safe and efficient operation of the enterprise" and that not adhering to the employment standard may have an extremely adverse financial impact.

Recruiting Procedures

We have already seen in Step 3 the necessity for expanding recruiting sources to include outreach organizations that specialize in the placement of minority personnel and women. (Appendix C lists several sources for recruiting minority group and women applicants, as well as some predominantly black colleges located throughout the United States that you may wish to consider for recruiting purposes.)

I also recommend the following recruiting procedures:

- Avoid recruiting primarily on the basis of employee referrals or "walk-ins." This method tends to perpetuate the present composition of a company's work force. Excessive reliance on such recruiting methods has been interpreted by the courts as a discriminatory practice.
- Use minority employees as recruiters and interviewers. In addition, send minority recruiters to high schools, colleges, job fairs, and minority recruiting centers, and include their photographs in recruiting programs and in consumer advertising campaigns.
- Seek out minority group and women leaders in the community. Inform them of employment opportunities in the company and request their active assistance in referring qualified candidates for employment consideration.
- Encourage minority group employees and women to refer their friends and relatives for jobs.
- Where applicable, use customer service centers in the minority community for recruiting purposes.
- Establish and maintain contact with employment counselors in schools with a large minority enrollment.

The Interview

Both the application form and the interview itself can inadvertently be the source of numerous violations of the law. Once again, it is strongly suggested that any inquiry put to the applicant, either on the application form or during the actual interview, pass the acid test of: (1) being specifically *job related* and (2) filling a true *business need*.

Although the final legal status of several questions that can be asked of the applicant is still to be determined by the courts, as a general rule, avoid asking for the following information:

- Applicant's race, national origin, or religion.
- Applicant's arrest record or credit rating.
- Charge accounts, home or car ownership, or life insurance that is carried.
- Marital status, number and ages of children, and their care arrangements.
- And in most instances, availability for Saturday or Sunday work (such a question may reveal a person's religious preference).

In addition, receptionists and all persons interviewing job candidates should be thoroughly informed on the requirements of the law and the organization's equal employment policies, and they should undergo an extensive interviewer training program. Moreover, they should be cautioned not to be biased by dress or grooming styles that may be unique to certain racial or ethnic groups, such as the popular Afro hairstyle.

Psychological Testing

Contrary to a popular misconception, the government and the courts have *not* ruled out the use of psychological tests in personnel selection. If anything, many organizations have found that properly designed and administered psychological tests have helped them in selecting better personnel, and that a professionally developed program has often been the *best* defense against charges of alleged employment discrimination. The "Guidelines on Employee Selection Procedures" released by the Equal Employment Opportunity Commission clearly state that ". . . properly validated and standardized (psychological tests) can significantly contribute to the implementation of non-discriminatory personnel policies. It is also recognized that professionally developed tests . . . may significantly aid in the development and maintenance of an efficient work force and, indeed, aid in the utilization and conservation of human resources generally."

It is not the purpose of this chapter to go into any great technical detail regarding the use of psychological tests in personnel selection. Suffice it to say that psychological testing is a highly specialized and complex field requiring the services of a professionally competent industrial psychologist. Moreover, it is vital to bear in mind that any test that adversely affects the employment status of minority personnel or women must be professionally validated ("testing the test") to determine that it is, in fact, a significant predictor of effective job performance. Such a validation procedure should be conducted by an experienced industrial psychologist, thoroughly familiar with current federal requirements in this area.

Step #7. Establish an Internal Audit and Reporting System to Evaluate the Effectiveness of the Company's Program

To determine the success of an organization's equal employment opportunity and affirmative action program, it is necessary to establish an internal audit and reporting system to monitor and to evaluate progress in each aspect of the program. Of particular significance in adhering to current equal employment opportunity requirements is the maintenance of *job applicant flow data.* More specifically, the government requires accurate and detailed records—

which must be retained for one full year—to be kept of each job applicant with regard to the following factors:

1. Date of application.
2. Name of applicant.
3. Specific minority group of which applicant is a member.
4. Applicant's sex.
5. Specific position applied for.
6. Appropriate equal employment opportunity category (i.e., officials and managers; professional; technicians; sales; office and clerical; craftsmen, skilled; operators, semiskilled; laborers, unskilled; service workers; apprentices and on-the-job trainees for production or white-collar positions).
7. Precise disposition of application for employment.
8. Recruiting source that referred the applicant.

Step #8. Organize Appropriate Additional Supportive Training and Development Programs

To further the process of equal employment opportunity, the government has strongly suggested that organizations develop a variety of additional supportive programs, among them the following:

- Training programs to inform supervisors and managers of their legal responsibilities as well as the organization's commitment to the principle of equal employment opportunity.
- Support services to assist minority personnel in personal counseling on financial, legal, transportation, health, housing, and child care matters.
- Job-related training programs to develop needed skills in minority personnel and women.
- Participation with other community organizations in the development of additional educational programs.

Also, because administrative guidelines and court interpretations frequently change over the course of time, personnel experts should keep themselves constantly up to date by subscribing to one or several of the legal reporting services that cover recent developments in the field. Companies that offer such reporting services are Prentice-Hall, Englewood Cliffs, N.J.; Commerce Clearing House, Chicago; and the Bureau of National Affairs, Washington, D.C.

three

Step 1—Determining accurate and realistic staffing specifications

BEFORE WE can even begin to think of filling a particular position that has become available in our organization, we must have a crystal clear picture of the job. This is the initial step that must precede all subsequent steps in my system; for example, contacting appropriate recruiting sources or writing a suitable newspaper help wanted advertisement. Unless we know the precise requirements of the position, we will not be able to give adequate guidance and direction to our recruiting sources—causing both them and us to waste time. If we are somewhat in the dark, or are generally nebulous regarding some of the essential aspects of the position, it is most unlikely that we will write the kind of help wanted ad that will attract enough well-qualified applicants from which to make a selection.

THE IMPORTANCE OF JOB ANALYSIS

Essentially, then, what we need at this stage in my Sequential Selection System is a detailed and accurate job description that includes such vital factors as duties to be performed, related working conditions, authority and reporting relationships, and any other important and pertinent aspects of the job. Once the job description has been obtained, we are ready to list the essential job specifications; that is, a compilation of the main qualifications an applicant must possess to carry out the duties and responsibilities of the position successfully. Many companies have found it useful to prepare a personnel requisition, both for administrative and control purposes and to provide the personnel department with the basic job information it needs. Job descriptions and job specifications are both end products of the process known as job analysis—a system that gathers critical basic information about a particular position.

JOB ANALYSIS AND EQUAL EMPLOYMENT OPPORTUNITY REQUIREMENTS

Job analysis as a personnel selection tool is by no means new. It gained a place as a standard personnel technique in the 1940s. Interestingly, however, a significant degree of renewed interest in the field of job analysis has emerged lately, primarily precipitated by the current emphasis on adherence to equal employment opportunity requirements. As the preceding chapter stressed, where the courts or a governmental investigative agency have found an employment practice or policy—as in this instance a job specification—to have an adverse impact upon a member of a protected class, or where such a policy or practice perpetuates the effect of previous discriminatory practices, with almost no exceptions it is illegal—unless the company can prove that such a job specification is absolutely essential because of business necessity.

In most instances the technique used to determine whether the policy or practice is legal is job analysis. If, for example, we need to justify using a typing or stenographic test on a job applicant seeking a secretarial position, a review of the *content* of the position in question should immediately support the use of the test to measure an indispensable skill for that particular job.

PERFORMING A JOB ANALYSIS

Job analysis, then, is the process by which significant information related to a particular job is obtained in a systematic and orderly fashion. Most standard textbooks in the field of personnel administration and industrial-organizational psychology can provide detailed information on this technique. Job analysis can be performed by

1. Observing an employee as he goes about performing his job.
2. Interviewing the incumbent regarding the nature of the job.
3. Administering job-related questionnaires to individuals doing the job.
4. A combination of several or all of the indicated techniques.

In many organizations, when a department wishes to fill a given position a duly approved personnel requisition is prepared and forwarded to the personnel department, authorizing it to set the staffing wheels into motion. Such a requisition (see Figure 1 for a sample personnel requisition form) usually contains the job analysis information necessary to guide the personnel department. If the information is missing or insufficient, or if the position is an entirely new one, the personnel specialist should seek out the ap-

Figure 1. Requisition for employment form, front.

REQUISITION FOR EMPLOYMENT		☐ WEEKLY ☐ STAFF

A | POSITION SPECIFICATIONS

JOB TITLE | JOB CODE

DIVISION | DEPT. | LOCATION

1. BRIEF DESCRIPTION OF DUTIES AND RESPONSIBILITIES: _____
(ATTACH JOB DESCRIPTION IF AVAILABLE)

| ☐ NEW POSITION ☐ REPLACEMENT FOR ____ | WHO HAS ☐ RESIGNED ☐ TRANFERRED TO ____ WAS ☐ TERMINATED ☐ OTHER ____ | STARTING SALARY RANGE | IS THIS REQUEST WITHIN YOUR APPROVED MANNING TABLE ☐ YES ☐ NO | ARE FACILITIES & EQUIPMENT AVAILABLE ☐ YES ☐ NO |

B | KNOW-HOW

1. EDUCATIONAL BACKGROUND:

DESIRABLE _____ MINIMUM _____

2. WORK EXPERIENCE:

DESIRABLE _____

MINIMUM _____

3. OTHER ATTRIBUTES DESIRABLE: _____

C | POSSIBLE AVENUES OF ADVANCEMENT

1. (WHERE CAN HE GO IF HE HAS THE ABILITY? INCLUDE TIME ESTIMATE WHERE PRACTICAL) _____

D | POSSIBLE SOURCES

1. WHAT DEPARTMENT(S) IN THE COMPANY COULD SUPPLY POTENTIAL CANDIDATES FOR THIS POSITION? _____

2. POTENTIAL EXTERNAL SOURCES _____

E | AUTHORIZATION

SIGNATURE	DATE	INTERVIEW REQUIRED	SIGNATURE	DATE	INTERVIEW REQUIRED
(SUPERVISOR)		☐ YES ☐ NO			☐ YES ☐ NO
SIGNATURE	DATE		SIGNATURE	DATE	
(DEPT. HEAD)		☐ YES ☐ NO	(DIVISION HEAD)		☐ YES ☐ NO

PERSONNEL USE ONLY

DATE RECEIVED	REQ. NO.	DATE FILLED
NAME OF EMPLOYEE		SOURCE

COMMENTS _____

Figure 1. Requisition for employment form, back.

PERSONNEL USE ONLY										
RECRUITING SOURCES										
ADVERTISING			PLACEMENT SERVICES			OTHER SOURCES				
NO. RESP	NAME	DATE	NO. RESP	NAME	DATE	NO. RESP	NAME		DATE	

INDIVIDUALS RECOMMENDED TO DEPARTMENT					
NAME	DATE	SOURCE	INTERVIEWED BY	FINAL ACTION	

DATE RECEIVED	REQ. NO.	NAME EMPLOYEE HIRED		☐ MALE ☐ FEMALE	DATE HIRED	DATE REPORT
POSITION TITLE		DEPT. TRANS. FROM	REPLACEMENT REQUIRED ☐ YES ☐ NO	STARTING SALARY	INTERVIEWER	

INSTRUCTIONS

A. USE OF FORM
This form will be used to request the Personnel Department to initiate a search for a employee.

B. PREPARATION AND PROCESSING
1. Prepare Request for Employee in duplicate, completing all information requested on the FRONT side of this form. If the section is not pertinent, note "Not pertinent to this position".
2. Circulate for approval as indicated under AUTHORIZATION (Item F)
3. Distribute the completed and approved forms as follows:
    a. Original - to Personnel Department.
    b. Copy   - to be retained by Originator.

propriate manager and obtain additional information. Moreover, since jobs are constantly changing in scope and requirements—particularly in an age of rapid social and technological change—it is important that the job information be kept up to date. In many companies all jobs are periodically reviewed to keep up with possible changes.

THE JOB DESCRIPTION

The first step in gathering pertinent job information is to prepare an accurate job description. Here we wish to obtain a dynamic and realistic picture of what the position entails. Probably of greatest importance in developing a job description is a comprehensive statement of the precise *duties* that are typically performed. Further information should be gathered on the following factors to round out our overall understanding of the position:

1. *Physical environment and related working conditions.* Will the job be performed in an office, a factory, or a shop? Is the work indoors or outdoors? Is it likely to be hot or cold? Will it be dusty, humid, or odorous? Are there any unusual or special physical or environmental aspects we should know about in recruiting suitable applicants?

2. *Equipment, machinery, or tools to be used.* With what equipment, machinery, or tools will the employee be working? Will he be using any special instruments, gauges, or apparatus in the course of performing his duties?

3. *Level of complexity and extent of responsibility and authority.* How difficult is the job? Is it fairly simple, or is it difficult or complex? What is the extent and nature of responsibility inherent in the position? How much authority will the person holding the job be expected to exercise?

4. *Degree of contact with the public or with customers.* What is the nature and degree of contact the person will have with other personnel within the organization? Will there be contact with the public, with customers, or possi-

bly with government officials? What are the extent, purpose, and possible ramifications of such contact?

5. *Access to confidential or competitive information.* Will the employee be working with confidential or competitive information, data, or reports? What is the degree of discretion the person will be expected to exercise in working with such privileged information?

6. *Extent of independent judgment and initiative required.* Will the person be expected to make decisions on his own, or is he more likely to carry out fairly routine and standardized instructions?

7. *Extent of supervision and direction received.* Is the supervision in the assignment fairly close and constant, or will the employee work pretty much on his own, with only indirect supervision from management?

8. *Extent of pressure.* Does the job entail stress or pressure, and if so, what is the nature and extent of the pressure?

9. *Extent of job structure.* Some jobs are clearly defined and highly structured and are subject to relatively little variability. Is the position fairly structured, or is there a high degree of ambiguity and uncertainty in the assignment where the person cannot rely on precedent or clearly prescribed company policies and procedures to guide him?

10. *Terms of employment.* What are the amount and method of compensation? What are the working hours? Will there be shift work, work on weekends, or work at night? Will there be travel or possible relocation?

11. *Any other special or significant features in the position.* Here we would want to learn any other special aspects or features of the job that would be important for an accurate and comprehensive picture.

JOB SPECIFICATIONS

Once we have obtained an accurate and complete picture of the position, we are ready to list the precise qualifications the successful candidate should possess. Without doubt, this is a key and critical step.

In the previous chapter, where we discussed equal employment opportunity requirements, we noted that to satisfy governmental regulations, job specifications must be directly job related and an organization must be prepared to substantiate that business necessity demands adherence to its stated specifications. To these two legal requirements, we would like to add a third requirement; namely, that specifications should also be realistic. All too often, in stipulating the requirements of a position, the frame of reference is unduly influenced by the present or last person who happened to have held the particular position. However, such a person may possess qualifications that exceed those actually required.

A person often fails in an assignment because he is overqualified, and finds the position insufficiently challenging. It certainly would not make any sense to hire a graduate accountant when the job calls for the services of a routine bookkeeper. Consequently, if we are to hire candidates who will be successful in the job—and if we are to avoid the high cost of personnel turnover—we must be equally sensitive to the risk of hiring candidates who may be overqualified or underqualified.

As an aid in determining which job specifications are truly realistic, I suggest that you identify the really *critical* requirements of the job. Certain credentials, qualifications, or personal characteristics are often nice to have, yet they may be completely superfluous. If you hire an applicant possessing such extras, you would obviously have to pay more than necessary, adding to your labor costs.

A particular incident that happened to me when I was a personnel executive will illustrate this situation. A sales manager once sent through a personnel requisition for a highly experienced secretary, insisting that she have stenographic skills approximating 120 words per minute.

On the basis of the requisition, a well-qualified applicant was hired who commanded a salary commensurate with her abilities.

Some months later, the secretary came into the personnel department explaining that, contrary to her original expectations, the sales manager was on the road two to three weeks per month. Instead of giving her a good deal of dictation, he sent her correspondence on hotel stationery written in longhand that he expected her to type up. The secretary announced that she was leaving the company because she feared that before too long she would lose the stenographic skills she had worked so hard to bring to a high level of proficiency. We can see here a clear-cut case of having an overqualified person and paying too much for unneeded skills on the basis of an unrealistic job specification.

Another method of identifying the truly critical factors in a position is to do a differential analysis of the qualifications possessed by employees who have been successful in the job against those who have failed in the particular assignment. Admittedly such a "success–failure" analysis requires a certain amount of effort and a commitment on the part of the organization in terms of time and money. However, it may frequently turn out to be exceedingly useful in empirically identifying important and vital applicant qualifications and serve a further purpose in helping a company to validate its job specifications for equal employment opportunity agencies.

IDENTIFYING ACCURATE AND REALISTIC JOB SPECIFICATIONS

In determining the truly essential job specifications to be taken into account, I would list the following five general categories: level of education, extent of prior work experience, specialized skills, level of intelligence, and essential personality characteristics.

Level of Education

How much education is really necessary? Will high school suffice, or is a college education really essential? Need the successful applicant have done postgraduate work? In what fields or course of study should he have specialized? What is the preferred or required major?

Extent of Prior Work Experience

What is the nature and type of previous experience the applicant should possess? How much prior experience is required? What is the level and extent of responsibility, authority, and decision-making experience the candidate should have had? What is the preferred prior work environment—one with a high or low degree of job structure?

Specialized Skills

Should the applicant bring to the job any specialized or technical skills? For example, how fast should the applicant be able to type? What stenographic speed is expected of the secretarial candidate? With what computer language should the programmer applicant be familiar? Should the machinist be able to set up his own machine? Must the technical administrative assistant be familiar with engineering or scientific terminology? A related question is whether there are any legal or statutory requirements an applicant must meet, such as state licensing or certification, as in the nursing profession.

Level of Intelligence

I have already suggested that a given candidate might fail in a certain assignment because he was overqualified. One way in which a person might easily be overqualified is that he could be too intelligent for the position. Some jobs make rather stringent mental demands, while others are fairly simple, routine, or repetitive in nature and fail to present enough of a challenge to a person with a higher degree of mental ability. The problem, then, is to determine the optimum or desired level of intelligence for the position.

Essential Personality Characteristics

A job may require some specific personality attributes. A careful review of the job description may show that a certain kind of personality is exceedingly desirable, if not absolutely indispensable. For example, an office receptionist should have an outgoing, extroverted, and friendly personality. Obviously, an extremely shy, introverted, or socially awkward person would not make a good receptionist, although he or she could no doubt perform well in another assignment, where such a personality trait would not in any way pose a handicap.

Since jobs vary widely in their demands and functions, a long list of personality traits could be rated. Among them we might list degree of physical energy, tendency to act in a deliberate and cautious fashion, personal initiative, creativity and imagination, behavior flexibility, tolerance for ambiguity and for job stress, self-confidence and self-assurance, decisiveness, analytical orientation, social bearing, personal projection, interpersonal effectiveness, individual assertiveness, competitiveness, and verbal articulation and spontaneity. The above characteristics are not all-inclusive but suggestive. From your own experience and knowledge of job requirements in your organization, you can undoubtedly add to this list.

Now that we have formulated a job description and have indicated the critical job specifications for the successful candidate, we are ready to go to Step 2 and contact selected recruiting sources to find enough well-qualified candidates from which to make our selection. This will be the subject of the next chapter.

four

Step 2—Effective applicant recruiting

To A GREAT EXTENT the success we achieve in hiring competent people is a direct result of how effective our recruiting program has been. It is obvious that the only people we will be able to hire are those who have been attracted to our organization—in essence, recruited as a result of our efforts. Potential candidates we have been unable to interest can never get on our payroll. Regrettably, many highly desirable people will never be considered for employment because we have been unable to get them to apply.

A personnel administrator may find that the job for which he is recruiting is difficult to fill and that few well-qualified candidates are available in the labor market who meet the company's traditional requirements. What often happens in such an instance is that after the vacancy has been open for a while, pressure starts to build up to fill it. The company may be tempted to compromise on its customary standards and employ a less qualified candidate than it would like. In the wake of subsequent events, that decision may be regretted later. However, at the time it is only human nature to rationalize that "if you can't get what you want, you must settle for what you can get."

This chapter is based on my experience that good people are usually hard to find in tight as well as in loose labor markets, and that if an organization is going to be successful in attracting qualified people, it must launch and maintain a vigorous, energetic, and imaginative recruiting program. There are exceptions and variations, of course. In our dynamic economy, conditions never remain precisely the same for very long. The economics of the labor market are such that personnel shortages in a given occupation today may quite readily turn to a surplus in relatively short order, and vice versa. For example, in recent years we have seen periods when the nation alternated shortages with surpluses in the number of engineering applicants. In the "soaring sixties" most companies complained that they were unable to recruit enough qualified college graduates for their various management training programs, but that shortage vanished rapidly with the advent of recession in 1974–1975.

At any one point there are usually paradoxes in the labor market. While I was writing this particular chapter, I was asked to meet with three groups of people, each of whom had a completely different and contrasting perception of the state of the labor market. The first two groups consisted of job seekers requesting assistance in helping them to find suitable employment. These people were either unemployed or underemployed. The first group consisted of school teachers and educational counselors, who indeed were facing a very discouraging job market. The second group consisted mostly of middle-level professional, technical, and managerial people seeking to improve their employment situation in a weak economy.

In contrast with these two groups was a team of marketing executives from a major company who wanted me to consult with them on specific ways they could improve the selection of their field sales force. Ironic as it may be, while the first two groups asked "Where are the jobs?" the marketing executives were asking, "Where are the applicants?"

Every personnel specialist has been confronted at one time or another in his career by a manager wanting to know why "With the newspapers writing about all the good people out of work, how come it's taking you so long to fill my particular job?" Actually, unemployment statistics as published by the government frequently are not particularly relevant or applicable to a specific company's personnel requirements. Generally, the people out of work in a community are not the same people who can fill existing vacancies in the company. In any given community, the labor market may simultaneously have shortages and surpluses in different occupational categories. Let us see, however, why in most instances well-qualified job candidates are so hard to come by.

WHY GOOD PEOPLE ARE HARD TO FIND

Barring unusual circumstances, qualified, capable job applicants are quite scarce and fairly hard to locate. Many managers find this personnel fact of life difficult to believe—and even more difficult to accept. One reason is that since they are not professional personnel administrators, they have not had first-hand experience with the staffing process. Moreover, many of them may be influenced by their own personal experiences in the past as a job seeker. What they predominantly remember is the difficulty they encountered in finding suitable employment. Consequently, they have a different perception of the employment process from that of the professional personnel specialist.

Why are good candidates such a rare commodity? Several explanations can be put forth. First, all organizations are eager to retain their productive and valuable employees. They have learned from their own experience that competent personnel are hard to come by. Therefore, they are most anxious to retain people who are making a useful contribution to the company. As a result, they will do their best to keep their present employees satisfied, challenged, and rewarded so as to minimize the possibility that they will be tempted to look elsewhere. Their employees, if they are kept happy, obviously will see no reason to leave the company. Consequently, whenever we initiate the recruiting process, our labor pool is already limited in terms of the number of possible job candidates who might be viable contenders for the position in question.

There are several other reasons for the scarcity of good job applicants. Since the end of World War II the United States has undergone a significant growth in its economy. Most companies have expanded dramatically. Even though the growth and expansion has been somewhat uneven and interrupted by dips in the economy and by periodic recessions, the total growth has been substantial. A concomitant of this growth has been the need for increasingly qualified personnel.

Many labor economists feel, also, that the trend toward decentralization has resulted in the need for additional personnel. They point out that business has recognized that a highly centralized structure often results in an unwieldy and unmanageable bureaucracy that contributes to inefficiency. However, in order to take advantage of the benefits of a decentralized operating structure, it is often necessary to employ more people.

Lastly, not only have business and industry grown and expanded dramatically, but we have seen a comparable growth in the nation's nonprofit sector. Included here are such not-for-profit institutions as hospitals, schools, and colleges; charitable, philanthropic, and social service organizations; and, of course, government service—federal, state, and local. At times segments of this part of the economy have grown even more rapidly than the profit sector. In essence, then, the personnel specialist can never become complacent in his recruiting efforts. If he does he will quickly find that he lacks a large enough pool of qualified applicants from which to make his final selection.

FUNDAMENTALS OF SUCCESSFUL RECRUITING

Most personnel administrators, at one time or another, have regretted that they were not able to select a better applicant for a particular opening. Occasionally, in filling a specific position, the personnel specialist may voice the opinion that the individual just hired was adequately, or perhaps minimally, qualified for the assignment. He was not of particularly outstanding caliber, however, and the personnel specialist may regret not being able to obtain a better candidate.

The best applicant of those who applied may have been hired. The problem was that not enough high-caliber applicants were attracted. This is a common complaint. Many companies have felt at times that they were not hiring quite the quality of employees they wanted. The problem may not have been faulty interviewing techniques. The company's recruiting strategy may have been inadequate. I cannot overemphasize the need to develop the type of recruiting program that will provide the company with a large number of highly desirable candidates, so that true selection can take place.

Let us consider some of the fundamentals of a good personnel recruiting program.

1. *A large number of well-qualified job applicants must be attracted.* It has been my experience, both as a person-

nel executive and as a management consultant, that it is absolutely imperative that a fairly large number of good applicants be recruited if an effective selection system is to operate. The personnel administrator cannot be selective enough in his choice of a candidate if he does not have a large applicant pool.

In this connection, I feel that one can never really have too many applicants for a given position. You may raise a very legitimate eyebrow at this statement. After all, you may say, I have definite restrictions of staff size and time within which to work. I could not function if too many applicants were to present themselves for any one position. In defense of my position I will demonstrate in the next chapter how applicants who do not meet the stipulated requirements can be screened out quickly.

It should be reiterated, however, that only candidates who *apply* can be considered for employment. People we have been unable to attract will never be viable contenders, no matter how desirable they may be. Their potential contribution to our company will never be realized. Therefore, as large an applicant pool as possible should be recruited.

2. *Never compromise on selection standards.* Closely related to the points made in the preceding section is the personnel maxim that one should never compromise or lower one's traditional selection standards. In practice, however, this principle is frequently violated—either consciously or unconsciously. More often than not it is difficult for the personnel specialist to come up with an applicant who meets all the stated employment standards. He may find himself with a number of requisitions in the same or a closely related job category, but with a dearth of qualified applicants.

The resultant pressure could cause him to lower his standards, rationalizing that "half a loaf is better than none," or that the urgency to fill the opening is so great as to necessitate a temporizing of customary standards. As we shall see in a later chapter, this is fundamentally a bad practice and should be strenuously avoided. Again, the best way to prevent such a situation from arising is to recruit enough applicants to make it totally unnecessary to compromise.

3. *Recruiting should be on a continuous and ongoing basis.* If a recruiting program is to provide a company with enough candidates for any given opening, it must be on a continuing basis. Most companies have found that they cannot be assured of enough well-qualified candidates unless they maintain an active and continuous recruiting program. It takes time for a company to establish a smoothly functioning, harmonious, and mutually productive relationship with its various recruiting sources. Recruiting simply cannot be turned on and off at will and still work effectively. If a satisfactory relationship with a recruiting source is suspended or permitted to lapse—say, because recruiting needs are less acute as a result of a temporary lull in the company's business—it will be difficult to reactivate the relationship once the company begins to move into higher gear again.

In this connection, it is suggested that a company maintain its contacts with the placement directors of the colleges and universities at which it has actively recruited personnel over the years. It should not permit the relationship to lapse simply because it does not plan to do any college recruiting during the current academic year. Even if a company anticipates no immediate need for recent college graduates, it might reconsider and add one or more individuals if they were of outstanding caliber and warranted being hired. The personnel administrator must remember that in maintaining his recruiting contacts, he is not merely assuring himself of high-quality referrals for today's openings, but, perhaps more importantly, he is building recruiting sources for tomorrow's needs.

Similarly, the personnel specialist will find that periodically a recruiting source will contact him to recommend that he interview a given applicant even though no opening exists at the moment. The person should be interviewed. At the very least his application or résumé should be obtained if there is even the slightest possibility that his services might be needed one day. Such an application, properly categorized and placed in a "hold" file for possible future use, enables the company to contact the individual if an appropriate position materializes. Many a personnel manager has had an application from just such a "rare bird" in his file and has been able to contact him promptly when the right job opened up.

4. *Recruiting should be creative, imaginative, and innovative.* Lastly, successful recruiting should have a certain flair and novelty. The personnel administrator should perceive himself as somewhat of a marketing specialist. As we shall see in a later chapter, a major part of successful recruiting is selling the company to a prospective applicant. Employment is a two-way street. The company must select the best possible candidate from a list of applicants. At the same time it must persuade a desirable candidate that his future career goals and objectives will be well served by joining the organization.

A creative, innovative, and imaginative recruiting program—one that is perceived by the job applicant as unique—can be highly successful in attracting a more qualified group of potentially promising employees. Some years ago, while working as a personnel executive, I conducted an informal survey of clerical and secretarial job applicants and asked them why, with all the many advertisements appearing in *The New York Times* help-wanted columns, they responded to my company's ad. The most frequent answer was that the ads were regarded by these applicants as different and imaginative. These ads made them decide to investigate my company's openings rather than those of other advertisers.

EFFECTIVE RECRUITING SOURCES

In the preceding section, we discussed some basic fundamentals of successful recruiting. We are now ready to explore in some depth the various recruiting sources that are available to the personnel administrator. Here is a checklist of selected recruiting sources.

1. Recommendations and referrals
2. Newspaper advertisements
3. Advertising in trade, professional, or business journals
4. Private employment agencies
5. Public employment services
6. High schools; trade and technical schools
7. Professional, sales, and business organizations
8. Recruiting at professional, technical, or business conventions
9. College recruiting
10. Executive search firms
11. Unsolicited ("walk-in") applicants
12. "Career centers"
13. Minority candidate and women career centers
14. Community organizations—e.g., Jaycees, the Y, women's clubs
15. Direct mail solicitation
16. Telephone recruiting

The list is not all-inclusive. No doubt you know of others. Nor is the list intended to imply any rank order of preference or relative superiority of one source over another. Instead, it should be regarded as a sampling of sources. Depending on your own local situation, you will probably find one or more sources preferable over others. Trial and error may be the only means for testing before deciding which source to use in the long run for a given type of job opening.

We shall begin this section by listing some recommended recruiting sources. Subsequently, more detailed comments will be provided for each of the following sources:

Private employment agencies
Newspaper advertising

Recommendations and referrals
Schools and colleges
Executive search firms
Unsolicited or "walk-in" candidates
Telephone recruiting
Other recruiting sources

Private Employment Agencies

The two most frequently used recruiting sources are private employment agencies and newspaper advertising. We will discuss the latter separately. There are many employment agencies located in virtually every city in the United States, but in my experience their quality leaves a good deal to be desired. This has been the general consensus on the part of an overwhelming number of participants at recruiting and selection workshops I have conduced throughout the country for many years. Still, properly used, the employment agency can save the personnel specialist a good deal of time. It can do a competent job of prescreening suitable candidates and referring only people who are truly qualified for further consideration. Employment agencies can be expensive. Fees are generally paid by the employer and usually approximate 10 percent of the candidate's starting salary. Nevertheless, a good employment agency can save a personnel administrator valuable time by screening out unqualified applicants and may therefore quite clearly be worth the cost. Furthermore, the company is only obligated to pay a fee after a qualified candidate has been hired.

In my opinion, however, there is a right way and a wrong way to work with private employment agencies. The agency field is a dynamic one. New agencies constantly open up while others go out of business. Furthermore, within the agencies themselves there are always numerous personnel changes as placement counselors leave one agency for another or go into business for themselves.

The personnel specialist should exercise a good deal of care in selecting the particular agencies with which he wishes to deal. It is a good idea to limit oneself to no more than three or four truly competent agencies, rather than attempt to work with virtually every agency in town and, as a result, probably not be properly serviced by any. Moreover, instead of identifying with a particular agency, it is far better to establish a strong business relationship with a specific placement counselor. If the person with whom you have been working leaves the agency to join another, it is advisable to continue the relationship with the same placement counselor at his new place of business.

In working effectively with an employment agency placement counselor, it is essential that he get to know you as an individual and, more importantly, that he acquire an in-depth understanding of your company, its business, and its employment standards and requirements. The better he understands your company's needs, the better a job he can do for you in screening out unqualified applicants and referring only qualified people.

Many personnel people have complained that agencies will flood them indiscriminately with totally unqualified job applicants. This seems to be endemic in the field. The best way to handle such a situation—which can waste everyone's time, particularly the personnel specialist's—is to be more selective in the choice of agencies with which you work and to insist that they adhere to the essentials of the job specification.

Another successful technique is to inform the placement counselor when you first list the opening that you will see only four or five applicants referred by him, and no more, and that you expect him to do a thorough screening job and to arrange for interviews only with those select few who, in his judgment, come closest to the specifications for the position. By using this technique, the personnel specialist will find that the placement counselor is more likely to be of true assistance to him and not waste his time.

Much of what has been said with respect to working effectively with private employment agencies applies equally well when dealing with the government-operated State Employment Service. In some parts of the country, personnel executives have met with excellent results in using this service, which, as a government agency, is free of charge to both employer and job applicant. Bear in mind, too, that if your company is a government contractor or subcontractor, you are required by law to list job openings with the local state employment office in compliance with the Vietnam Era Veterans' Re-Adjustment Assistance Act of 1974.

Newspaper Advertising

Help-wanted advertising is relatively inexpensive and a quick way to recruit applicants. Some companies greatly prefer this source over employment agencies. It avoids having to pay an agency's fee. If a company is expanding and hiring a considerable number of people, the fee costs can be substantial. At the same time, however, advertising can attract many unqualified applicants. If the ad calls for candidates to apply in person, the Personnel Department will have to spend a lot of time screening out unsuitable people. Furthermore, no matter how well the ad has been written, there is no guarantee that it will draw enough qualified applicants. Nevertheless, help-wanted advertising unquestionably remains one of the most popular and most effective ways of recruiting job applicants.

Most help-wanted ads appear in daily and Sunday newspapers. Lower level positions are customarily listed in the classified columns, while professional, managerial, and technical openings are generally displayed on the financial page. Sometimes, too, ads recruiting such people as engineers, designers, or electronic data processing personnel appear in the sports section.

At times, a company is interested in attracting as large a group of applicants as possible. Accordingly, it will highlight its opening with a prominent display ad, but will also run a small ad in the classified section referring the reader to the financial page. In recruiting for highly technical personnel, journals or magazines that are published by the nation's leading professional, scientific, and scholarly associations and societies are used. However, this method has a serious drawback. Journals have a fairly advanced publication deadline. Therefore, it takes a long time before the ad appears and responses begin coming in.

At the beginning of this chapter, creative and innovative techniques were encouraged to assure the success of recruiting efforts. They are particularly desirable when writing the newspaper help-wanted ad. If the ad is to attract a satisfactory number of good applicants, it must be imaginatively and well written, display a certain flair and excitement, and generate definite and positive interest on the part of the reader. Most major cities have advertising agencies that specialize in classified and display help-wanted ads. These advertising agencies can help a company write an interesting ad and insert it in any newspaper or magazine in the country. One well-known advertising agency's suggestions for writing an effective recruitment ad appear in Figures 2 and 3.

The personnel specialist may be able to write as good as—or even better than—the agency because of his intimate and first-hand knowledge and "feel" of his own organization. In any case, he should probably collaborate with the advertising agency in order to come up with a series of successful ads that generate an appropriate applicant flow, particularly since there is no charge for this service. The agency receives its commission directly from the newspapers themselves.

Figure 4 shows five fictitious ads and an actual one used by The Service Bureau Company. These ads, in my opinion, tend to attract attention and are likely to generate definite interest on the part of the potential or actual job seeker. Note the use of key, catchy headings and attention-getting expressions that cause the ads to stand out and be set apart from the bulk of help-wanted ads for similar positions. Some of the same effect can be obtained by the use of additional white space or by an outstanding layout. The following personal experience will underscore the importance of novelty in writing help-wanted advertising.

A number of years ago, I was a personnel executive with a major New York City-based corporation undergoing significant expansion. Because of the rapid growth of the company, it was necessary to conduct a vigorous and aggressive recruiting program for office personnel. It was found that the most effective way to recruit clerical and secretarial employees at a time when most organizations in New York were also expanding their operations and hiring was to use catchy, attention-getting headings in help-wanted advertising.

At that time, the most popular show on Broadway was "My Fair Lady," tickets to which were well-nigh impossible to obtain. Consequently, it was decided that in our classified ads we would use as an attention-getting device the caption "Want Two Tickets to My Fair Lady?" In the body of the ad we continued to say, of course, that we did not have any tickets to the show. However, we did have some interesting positions we were eager to discuss with qualified applicants.

We were exceedingly gratified by the large number of high-caliber candidates that applied and conducted an informal survey to find out why these people responded to our ad among so many. The answer was that the applicants were impressed by the uniqueness and good humor of our ads and therefore wanted to investigate precisely what opportunities the company did have to offer.

While on the subject of the actual wording of the help-wanted ad, I would like to include a few other suggestions for your consideration. It is better to use an "open"—that is, a signed—ad in which the company identifies itself than a "blind" one in which the advertiser's identity is unknown and the job seeker is asked to send a letter or résumé to a

A typical display-type recruitment ad is shown on this page, with its various elements and their functions labelled for easy identification. Classified recruitment ads comprise essentially the same elements, except for those relating to art work, and the limitation on type faces used in a particular newspaper's classified section.

*Figure 2. Elements of a recruitment ad. From the DS&E
Recruitment Manual 1976–1977. © 1976 by Deutsch, Shea
& Evans, Inc., New York. Used with permission.*

(A) **Key:**

1) Attracts attention of readers with training or experience indicated. 2) Screens out unqualified people. 3) Identifies ad as recruitment ad. ("Key" not always necessary for display ad in recruitment section of publication).

(B) **Headline:**

1) Attracts reader, motivates to read ad. 2) Summarizes ad message. 3) Screens out non-qualified.

(C) **Main subhead:**

1) Supplements headline. 2) Reinforces impact, and/or 3) Introduces a second motivating factor (Not all ads need subheads).

(D) **Illustration:**

1) Gains reader's attention. 2) Supports headline, and/or 3) Visually defines job, field or industry, and/or 4) Supplements ad message with non-verbal information (e.g. example shown demonstrates affirmative action). Not all display ads need illustrations.

(E) **Display type:**

1) Creates impact and visibility. 2) Makes headline easy to read. 3) Enhances attractiveness of ad.

(F) **White space:**

1) Isolates elements of ad for greater visual impact. 2) Enhances attractiveness and readability by avoiding cramped appearance.

(G) **Body copy (or text):**

1) Supports main message. 2) Expands on points made in headline and/or subhead. 3) Provides information on opportunities, company and field to motivate reader action.

(H) **Body type:**

Presents text of ad in readable form.

(I) **Subheads:**

1) Divide text for better readability. 2) Maintain reader interest in message, or 3) Introduce particular section of ad.

(J) **Job specifications:**

(Unique to recruitment ads) 1) Identify as recruitment ad. 2) Describe job openings and requirements (Sometimes simply a listing of job titles).

(K) **Contact information:**

Provides source for further information, where to forward resume, etc.

(L) **Affirmative action line:**

Assures potential applicants of company's compliance.

(M) **Logo:**

Company's official signature. 1) Identifies organization. 2) Attracts reader's attention if company is well known. 3) Builds company image.

Figure 3. Creative aspects of recruitment advertising: a checklist. From the DS&E Recruitment Manual 1976–1977. © 1976 by Deutsch, Shea & Evans, Inc., New York. Used with permission.

Judging from the employment sections of most publications, a majority of companies are content with recruitment ads that are dull and one-dimensional. A growing number of companies, however, have discovered that recruitment ads that are interesting and attractive are also more effective. They stand out on a page and generate more attention and thus more response. Often the response is from a higher caliber applicant. And not infrequently, some of these applicants appear long after the ad has run because the impression of the company it created has lasted over a substantial period. There is no ready formula for developing effective and creative recruitment advertising, but listed below are some of the considerations that can contribute toward this goal.

I. The Functions of a Recruitment Ad

Given the rising costs of advertising, it is to a company's advantage to get as much return as possible for its investment. A good recruitment ad can—and should—serve at least four functions.

A. **The ad should generate qualified inquiries** by reaching and motivating the particular audience from which the company can get the people it seeks; this is the primary function of recruitment advertising.

B. **It should create favorable employer image** at the same time. Research indicates some 75% of a publication's readers read recruitment ads regularly, whether or not they are seeking jobs. A good ad will make a long-lasting impression on this group.

C. **Your recruitment ads should have a positive effect on present employees,** who are among the most interested readers. Good ads confirm their own choice of employer, contribute to morale and cut turnover.

D. **Recruitment advertising should enhance the company image** among audiences important to it, since it is a form of corporate communication seen by stockholders, customers, potential investors, suppliers and many other groups.

II. The Criteria of a Creative Recruitment Ad

A. **Interest:** is there a feeling of news urgency in the ad? is the approach fresh? does the headline have a strong impact that will attract reader attention? does the ad's story maintain interest? does it avoid cliches?

B. **Information:** does the ad provide enough information about the nature of the job? does it tell who the company is and what it does? does it cover such areas as advancement, growth and other important career aspects?

C. **Viewpoint:** is the ad written in terms of the reader's interests? does it tie in company achievements and prospects with the career needs and aims of the reader? does it avoid appearance of continually extolling company?

D. **Believability:** does the ad document its claims? does it provide facts, data, examples to back up statements—avoid exaggerations, sweeping claims and glittering generalities?

E. **Uniqueness:** does the ad zero in on the advantages and characteristics unique to your company? or is it so general that any other company's name could as easily fit at the bottom of the ad? does the reader see how your company differs from others in its field?

F. **Visual functionality:** can the ad compete for reader attention based on size and appearance? does the visual element relate to the advertising message? is the design fresh? does it provide a news element? are elements unified and comfortable to the eye, rather than disparate and cramped?

G. **Human element:** does the ad sound and look as if it is directed to individual people? does it avoid being too slick and "Madison Avenue"? does it achieve a personal and human tone?

H. **Action orientation:** does it have a clear-cut call to action? does it provide the reader with the information necessary to take action?

Figure 4. Effective recruitment ads.

Would this situation intimidate you or motivate you?

The people we are looking for would be motivated by the opportunity to convey their ideas to the President of a Fortune 500 Company. They would not view him as a fire breathing dragon, but rather as a policy maker and a man who makes decisions. Therefore, when you are marketing a service such as ours, he's the right man to see.

We're not suggesting that it would be easy. On the contrary it's a difficult assignment and not everyone is qualified to handle it. That's why we become very selective when we decide to add to our marketing team.

You must have a proven record of achievement in business, education or the military service and a confidence that goes beyond your years. You must be subtle yet bold, aggressive yet tactful. You must want to help top executives define problems . . . and present solutions—much like a consultant.

Our successful Time-sharing Marketing Representatives have come to us from a diverse range of educational and business backgrounds; from

Finance to Science and from Sales to Education.

We are The Service Bureau Company, pioneers in the management time-sharing industry. An industry that has literally boomed in the last decade. Our growth has been both dynamic and sure. All forecasts for the future see an increased demand for the services we provide to the international business community.

We are an equal opportunity employer with positions currently available throughout the U.S.

We would like to know more about you, and we're sure you'd like to know more about us. Drop us a resume or a brief letter. Today.

The Service Bureau Company

SBC
Director of Marketing
Management Time-sharing
500 West Putnam Avenue
Greenwich, Conn. 06830
A Division of Control Data Corporation

From the Service Bureau Company, a division of Control Data Corporation. Used with permission.

Effective recruitment ads.

Draftsmen
Designers
Engineers

FIND OUT HOW YOU CAN SPARK YOUR CAREER AT
Consolidated Engineering, Inc.

WE'RE HAVING AN OPEN HOUSE SATURDAY

JAN. 29
9:00 AM to 5:00 PM

DESIGNERS & DRAFTSMEN

· MECHANICAL
·   High pressure piping design and layout. Knowledge ASME codes.
· ELECTRICAL
    Physical layout and wiring.
· STRUCTURAL
    Reinforced concrete drafting.

ENGINEERS

ENTRY LEVEL, SENIOR, LEAD, SUPERVISING, and PROJECT ENGINEERING positions for qualified Engineers with power plant experience.

· ELECTRICAL, MECHANICAL
· BUILDING SERVICE
· INSTRUMENTATION
· CIVIL NUCLEAR
· PLANNING SCHEDULING
· QUALITY CONTROL

Be sure to stop in next Saturday, Jan. 29, to discuss your career potential with this dynamic company . . . where your professional expertise and serious desire for growth and advancement will be recognized and rewarded. We're growth oriented, people oriented, and offer the careerist almost unlimited opportunities as part of our Power team.

Stop in Saturday, Jan. 29, or send your resume in advance to M. Duane Consolidated Engineering, Inc. Route 4, Linden, N.J. 07669

(An Equal Opportunity Employer)

SECRETARIES

Dear Secretaries:

If you've come into 1977 with a "ho-hum" job in a drab office, this could be a real Happy New Year letter for you.

I'm in the Personnel Department of Harrison & Smith, a prominent advertising agency located on Madison Avenue. And RIGHT NOW I have several great secretarial positions open.

How would you like to be the secretary of one of our Senior Executives, one of our top Copywriters, or one of our dynamic Account Executives? Each position has plenty of challenge, working for one person, and carries the excellent starting salary and the many benefits you'd expect.

If you have good steno and typing skills, and want more than just a job, call me weekdays between 9 and 4 at 696-8000.

Yours truly,
Ken Shields

(an equal opportunity employer)

KEYPUNCH OPERATORS
Here It Is........................The

WORST

JOB

IN

N.Y.C.!

LOW SALARY

LOUSY BENEFITS

This is a real nightmare of a job. Crummy offices. Terrible boss. ½ hour lunch. Never a day off. Everything, in fact, to make your life truly miserable. To find out more about this uninteresting opportunity, stop by this week. It may be the biggest mistake you ever made.

Contact Steve Harris

EDP DATA SERVICES
500 Fifth Ave. (42 St.)
945-6870

(an equal opportunity employer)

Effective recruitment ads.

box number in care of the newspaper. The job applicant usually wants to know to which company he is responding. The advertiser may be a company he does not wish to join or, as has happened on more than one occasion, it could be his very own employer! An open ad, therefore, invariably generates a greater number of responses than a similar one in which the advertiser's identity is not revealed.

Should the personnel specialist wish to move rapidly to fill an opening, he should ask the applicant to apply in person instead of writing a letter to the company. This more direct strategy is also recommended when filling lower level assignments; for example, at the clerical, secretarial, and factory level. In some instances, when time is of the essence, companies have found it advantageous to have the applicant telephone immediately for an early appointment.

Personnel departments should occasionally consider extending their customary interviewing hours beyond 5 P.M. one or two days a week to make it more feasible for the employed job applicant to schedule an interview. Frequently such candidates are of high quality, but because they are working they find it hard to break away during the regular interviewing hours. For higher level positions, on the other hand, the personnel specialist may request the applicant to send in a résumé or letter fully outlining his qualifications so that the material can be carefully reviewed before he decides which applicants he would like to invite in for a personal interview.

Lastly, be cautioned that in writing the newspaper ad you must not inadvertently violate any of the equal employment opportunity laws or court rulings. For example, as I stressed in the chapter on equal employment opportunity requirements, stating a preference for either sex or indicating a maximum age is illegal and likely to subject the company to penalties unless a bona fide occupational qualification can be successfully defended. Companies should be careful in their ads not to use such preferential expressions or words as the following: young man, gal Friday, boy, girl, recent college grad, salesman, or draftsman. All of them have been held to be in violation of equal employment opportunity laws. Instead, the personnel specialist should limit himself to a precise statement of the actual job specifications, which were discussed in the preceding chapter. Furthermore, toward the bottom of each ad, he should add the phrase "An Equal Opportunity–Affirmative Action Employer—M/F."

Recommendations and Referrals

Probably one of the best recruiting sources available to the personnel administrator is people already familiar with the company. Past and present employees, customers, vendors, contractors and suppliers, and sometimes even stockholders, may recommend applicants. The quality of applicants recommended by people who know the company and its standards and requirements is usually of a higher level than, for example, that of candidates coming from a totally unscreened source, such as a newspaper ad. The referred candidate can be considered a reflection on the person who recommended him. Therefore, people tend to be selective in referring applicants to the company.

Some companies have found it helpful, especially during periods of tight labor shortages, to encourage applicant referrals by their present employees by awarding them a cash payment whenever someone recommended by them is hired. Don't rely too much on such recommendations and referrals, however, particularly if the company's present employees are predominantly white. Their referrals might perpetuate the current composition of the work force and inadvertently violate equal employment opportunity requirements.

Schools and Colleges

Schools and colleges can serve as an excellent source of applicants for most organizations. Some companies have developed a very close relationship with neighborhood high schools that are able to supply them with a continuous flow of well-trained clerical and secretarial applicants on graduation. Similarly, industrial organizations have found that factory applicants, candidates for apprenticeship programs, and technical personnel are apt to be referred by trade and vocational schools with which they have maintained contact. More recently we have seen the emergence of college recruiting as a major professional activity. Most large organizations maintain a separate college relations function and conduct extensive recruiting programs at the undergraduate, graduate, and professional levels.

It takes time to develop an effective and mutually beneficial relationship with schools and colleges; it cannot be built up overnight. The educational institution must get to know the company and its personality and requirements so that only reasonably qualified candidates will be referred.

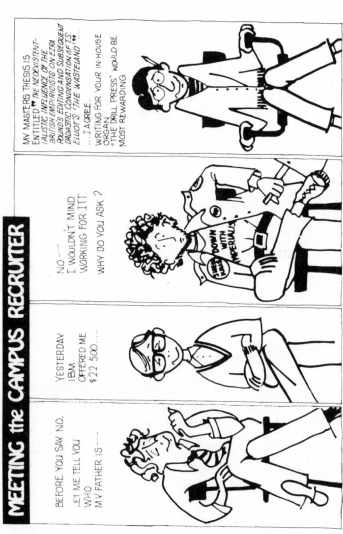

From *Personnel Forum*, Vol. 1 (April 1974). Bernard Hodes Advertising, Inc., New York. Used with permission.

For its part, the company can help facilitate its relationship with the school or college through such activities as making informative literature about the company available; offering summer, co-op, or field work employment to students (and sometimes to the faculty as well); and providing speakers for various educational programs, such as for senior day and career conferences.

Executive Search Firms

Executive recruiting firms have proliferated around the country and have become a key source for organizations seeking managerial, executive, and professional candidates. The basic reason for the growth in this field is that customary recruiting techniques rarely work successfully at this level. By and large, qualified executives and highly competent professional personnel do not respond to newspaper advertisements. Nor are they likely to apply to employment agencies. At the executive level, the job usually seeks out the man rather than vice versa.

Competent executive recruiting firms generally initiate their search by conducting a thorough and comprehensive analysis of their client's needs. When they arrive at a precise formulation of the specifications of the assignment, they engage in a broad and active campaign to identify and to seek out interested individuals who appear to fit the company's requirements. These people are then discreetly and confidentially referred to the company for its subsequent evaluation and consideration.

Unsolicited or "Walk-In" Candidates

Most organizations attract a certain number of job applicants who, on their own initiative, contact the company to inquire whether a suitable opening may exist for them. Depending upon the general reputation of the company as a desirable place in which to work, some organizations may find that a fairly large number of prospective employees apply in this manner. Many organizations have found that they are able to fill a lot of their lower level and even some relatively higher level positions this way.

Therefore, even if no immediate position exists when someone makes an inquiry, have that person fill out an application and file it for possible future use. At the same time, however, in order not to violate any of the equal employment opportunity laws, a company should be careful not to place excessive reliance on this recruiting source, particularly if it is located in a predominantly white area and most "walk-in" candidates tend to fall into this particular category.

Telephone Recruiting

A novel variation in using newspaper help-wanted advertising to attract applicants is a technique that, for lack of a better term, we shall call the "Telephone Recruiting Technique." While most newspaper ads ask the reader to apply in person or to submit a letter or résumé, the telephone recruiting technique uses a more direct approach. It invites the candidate to call in to obtain further information about the job and to be considered for the position. This technique, originally pioneered by Dr. Robert N. McMurry,* who calls it the "Sunday Special," has enjoyed a good measure of popularity and has been used successfully by many companies in filling a wide variety of openings—frequently openings that are difficult to fill because of a scarcity of high-caliber applicants.

What makes the telephone recruiting technique so effective is its simplicity and the ease with which the applicant can establish quick contact with the company. In essence, all he has to do is pick up the telephone. By this very act the recruiting process is set into motion. One explanation of the success of this technique is that it attracts not only the unemployed applicant, but also a relatively large number of employed and generally contented candidates who ordinarily would not respond to the traditional help-

* Robert N. McMurry, *How to Recruit, Select and Place Salesmen.* The Dartnell Corporation, 1964.

wanted ad because they are not really in the job market. Moreover, employed people do not as a rule have the time or inclination to apply for jobs in person, as they must if they answer most ads. Furthermore, since they are not actively seeking new employment, they ordinarily do not have a résumé readily available, and are not in a frame of mind to sit down and write a letter. However, as some of the sample ads that use the telephone recruiting technique illustrate in Figure 5, the ad itself may be attractively written. If it is, a fairly large number of qualified people will pick up the phone.

In using the telephone recruiting technique, the personnel specialist should write the ad in such a way as to list the essential specifications for the particular position clearly. More often than not, the ad will appear in the Sunday or weekend edition of the newspaper, inviting the reader to "Call Today, Sunday" (when the person is traditionally at home, presumably relaxed, and with the time to make the inquiry conveniently). However, many companies have found that the technique also works quite well if candidates are asked to call during business hours.

Let us see how this technique operates in practice. When the reader telephones to obtain more information, the recruiter should use a prepared, structured interview screening form to determine whether the caller possesses the basic qualifications needed to fill the position. Such a screening form should ask questions about the applicant's specific qualifications, and should have space provided on the form itself so that the recruiter can fill in the applicant's answers. For example, typical, critical, "make or break" questions might be:

1. What (accounting, sales, data processing) experience have you had?
2. What is your educational background?
3. What are your salary requirements?
4. Are you available for travel (relocation)?
5. Do you have a valid driver's license?

Figure 5. Ads used in telephone recruiting. From The McMurry Company, Chicago. Used with permission.

PERSONNEL DIRECTOR

Prestige national textile specialty in chemical processing company seeks Personnel Manager to develop program in its Arkansas plant (400 employees). Opportunity for growth into line management.

Must have minimum five years experience in personnel and labor relations. Salary open.

For personal, confidential interview, phone James S. Arnold (person-to-person, collect) Area 214, Riverside 7-7063, at Dallas, Texas. TODAY, SUNDAY, OR MONDAY (July 17-18), between 10:00 a.m. and 6:00 p.m.

EXECUTIVE VICE PRESIDENT

Homebuilders Association of Greater St. Louis

Capable, knowledgeable Executive Vice President is needed by the Greater St. Louis Association of Homebuilders. Must have the ability to participate actively in setting and fulfilling the Association's goals, but also to weld this diversified group of strong-minded entrepreneurs (250 builders, and 400 associate members) into a unified, constructive force. In addition, the Executive Vice President will represent the Association to the public; to government officials, hearings, etc.; and to the press, radio and TV.

Desirable background for this position would include college graduation, successful administrative experience, and some public relations work. Salary dependent upon qualifications, plus expenses.

For information, call Mr. Victor TODAY, Sunday, or Monday, between 10:00 a.m. and 5:00 p.m. at 944-0447.

GENERAL MANAGER

National technical electronics distributor with headquarters in San Francisco, now expanding to manufacturing assembly, seeks an experienced General Manager for a new electro-connector facility in Chicago. Will be responsible for the effective and profitable operation and growth of the Division and will report to the President of the Corporation. The position entails a large degree of autonomy and requires a self-starter with ability to conceive, formulate and implement programs.

Must have experience in managing a manufacturing activity, involving production, quality control, order processing, and marketing. Experience in electrical/electronic connectors and their assembly preferable.

Salary open; liberal incentive program, including profit sharing plan, with opportunity for stock options.

For information, call John Rogers, TODAY, Sunday, between 10:00 a.m. and 5:00 p.m., or Monday at 944-0445.

If the applicant's answers do not match the specifications for the position, the telephone interview can be terminated quickly. On the other hand, if the caller's qualifications correspond closely with the job specifications, the recruiter should ask for the candidate's name, address, and telephone number and indicate to him that he may be contacted during the next few days to arrange for a personal interview. If the applicant's qualifications appear to be exceptionally desirable, the telephone recruiter may wish to expedite the process by arranging an interview appointment immediately.

Many companies have found this technique to be exceedingly effective and to have worked well for them when other and more conventional recruiting strategies failed. By virtue of the ease with which applicants can "throw their hats into the ring"—after all, they need only telephone—candidates can be attracted who otherwise would probably not have made themselves available.

Other Recruiting Sources

Some additional recruiting sources you might want to consider include:

1. Placement services operated by local or community organizations, such as the Y, sales executives clubs, and Jaycees.
2. Professional societies and trade or business associations.
3. Recruiting at technical or professional conventions and meetings.
4. Direct solicitations to candidates known to the recruiter to be qualified.
5. Participation in community-sponsored career centers or in an "operation hometown."
6. Specialized minority and women's recruiting sources (see Appendix for the names and addresses of some representative organizations).
7. Internal job posting inviting current employees to apply for consideration.

five

Step 3—Initial applicant screening

ONCE WE HAVE attracted a number of promising job applicants, we have to identify those candidates who deserve our serious attention and screen out the others. I cannot overemphasize the importance of screening out the unqualified applicants properly. Many personnel practitioners and managers who do their own hiring spend far too much time interviewing job applicants who are completely unqualified. Essentially, this phase of my Sequential Selection System is again offering the opportunity to "work smarter, not harder."

Whenever we launch an effective recruiting program, we attract—as is our intention—a fairly large number of job applicants. Also, if our company is known as a good place to work, many unsolicited or "walk-in" individuals will inquire about the possibilities of employment. It is not at all

unusual for the vast majority of these candidates to be totally unqualified for the position for which they are applying. Nevertheless, since they are on the company's premises, they must be seen and interviewed by a representative of the organization.

Some applicants are not only unqualified but also highly
undesirable. Every personnel specialist has his favorite
anecdotes or "horror stories" of undesirable or difficult applicants who have appeared in the employment office,
sometimes even causing a mild disturbance. I myself have
encountered applicants who were intoxicated or under the
influence of drugs; were suffering from very serious and
obvious emotional disturbances; or were exceedingly hostile, belligerent, and antagonistic.

Such potentially troublesome—and sometimes explo-
sive—people must be promptly but tactfully sent on
their way so that they do not interrupt or disturb the customary functions and decorum of the employment office.
They should not be accorded lengthy interviews. However,
they should be seen promptly, and have the satisfaction of
knowing that the company has given their qualifications
proper consideration. We shall see shortly how this objective can be accomplished.

IMPORTANT CONSIDERATIONS IN
APPLICANT SCREENING

It is vital and only proper that every applicant be treated
fairly and courteously. This includes troublesome and
psychologically disturbed individuals whom the interviewer admittedly may find extremely trying and more
difficult to handle. Certainly, the customary principles of
effective interpersonal relations demand that we handle
every person with tact and sensitivity, but it is basically also
good business to do so. Many companies are in the public
eye and may, in fact, sell directly to consumers. Therefore,
nothing whatsoever can be gained from antagonizing or of-
fending a job applicant. Also, the applicant who is rejected

but remains positively disposed toward the company by virtue of the courteous treatment he has received may recommend another person who is better qualified and who might subsequently be hired.

Furthermore, in instituting an effective employment system, including a viable strategy for screening out the unqualified, we must continually exercise a great amount of care to see that we do not inadvertently violate any of the equal employment opportunity requirements. Nevertheless, some companies are so concerned that they might violate one of the EEO caveats that they spend an endless amount of time with each and every job applicant to avoid giving anyone the impression that he has been slighted. This is a great tactical error.

THE SCREENING INTERVIEW

I have found that initial applicant screening can best be accomplished through the perfected use of the screening, or mini-, interview. Basically, two purposes are served by the screening interview: (1) to determine whether the applicant possesses the critical specifications for the position in question; and (2) tactfully and gracefully to expedite the departure of unqualified applicants and those who are socially undesirable, overtly hostile, or emotionally disturbed.

The screening interview is not intended to elicit any real depth of background information from the job applicant, nor should it be construed in any way as a final selection interview. Its main purpose is to determine whether the applicant warrants further consideration. Properly used, it can save the personnel professional a tremendous amount of time. It usually takes no more than a few minutes. Some personnel specialists erroneously believe that they are morally obligated to give a lengthy, "full" interview to each and every job applicant. This is a time-consuming strategy that should be avoided at all costs.

Others feel insecure and uncomfortable conducting a

relatively brief interview, fearing that it is a telltale sign of rejection. This is a highly subjective feeling. Clearly, if the screening interview has been properly conducted, the applicant does not detect or sense that he has been rejected. After all, he is not familiar with the company's employment procedures; he simply does not know how the company operates.

Applicants realize that the personnel specialist is seeing a good many people and cannot give too much time to each and every candidate. Furthermore, they are aware that they have only had a preliminary interview, and that if further discussion is warranted, they will hear from the company again.

HOW TO CONDUCT THE SCREENING INTERVIEW

Let us see how the screening interview works in actual practice. I find that most often one or more of four approaches may be used to screen out unwanted job applicants. These screening strategies are:

1. Visual screening
2. Using critical or "knockout" questions
3. Reviewing the application form
4. Briefly describing the job to the applicant

We shall discuss each of these screening strategies in greater detail in the following sections.

Visual Screening

At times, merely looking at a candidate—sight screening, if you will—can suggest to the personnel professional that here is a totally unqualified candidate. Visual screening assistance can also be provided by a well-trained and perceptive receptionist who will alert the personnel specialist that one or several job applicants waiting for an interview are probably not qualified. These people should be seen promptly—not necessarily in order of arrival—and dispatched rapidly.

I have encountered exceedingly hostile people who tore up application forms when requested to complete them by a receptionist; people under the influence of alcohol; people suffering from serious emotional problems; people who even diapered their infant babies on a long table in the center of the personnel department placed there to enable candidates to complete their application forms; and, in one memorable instance, a belligerent applicant who was accompanied by two snarling and seemingly vicious attack dogs! Less dramatic examples of applicants who can be identified visually as warranting no more than a screening interview are those whose appearance and dress are entirely unacceptable; i.e., they are dirty, slovenly dressed, or unshaven.

The screening interview is intended to send the undesirable individual on his way quickly. Where initial visual screening is done by the receptionist, it is the personnel specialist's function to confirm or reject the receptionist's impressions. If the personnel interviewer does not concur with the receptionist's evaluation, he or she can still make arrangements to accord the applicant a more extensive interview later.

In conducting the screening interview, the personnel specialist should call the applicant's name and, if he so desires, actually conduct a brief "stand-up" interview with the candidate in the corridor, at a distance somewhat removed from the main reception area. He should not feel obligated to invite the applicant into his office. If his office is the only practical place to go, the personnel specialist may still wish to conduct a stand-up interview near his desk to convey the message to the applicant that this is only a preliminary meeting and that, if it appears appropriate, further and more intensive interviews will be scheduled later on.

Even if the applicant is obviously undesirable, the personnel specialist must go through certain motions. In such a case, it is suggested that the interviewer make conversation of sorts—for a few minutes at most—asking the candidate questions related to his past experience and current career goals and objectives. (See the list of Tested Questions that appears as Appendix A.) Very promptly thereafter, however, the applicant should be thanked for his interest in the company and told that other candidates will be interviewed within the next few days. He should be informed that if the company decides to give his application further consideration, it will be in touch with him by mail or by telephone. To avoid ambiguity, the interviewer should name a specific cutoff date, indicating that if the applicant has not heard from the company by that time, he should assume that a more qualified individual has been selected for the position. This strategy usually avoids having the applicant return to the company to inquire about the status of his application.

The interviewer must appear sincere, friendly, and interested in the applicant, difficult as that may be on occasion. In addition, he or she must be able to convince the candidate that he has been given full consideration. No applicant should ever be rejected or told that he is not qualified during the course of the screening interview. The interviewer might end up in a lengthy, unproductive debate. It is far better to tell the applicant that he is under consideration, along with other candidates for the job.

Using Critical or "Knockout" Questions

Most jobs have specifications that are absolutely critical. If the candidate lacks these qualifications, it is immaterial how well motivated or well intentioned he may be, or what other positive qualities he may possess. A lengthy interview is unnecessary. The screening interview can determine very quickly that he is not in the running.

This type of screening interview can be conducted by asking key or knockout questions of the applicant. The method is similar to the telephone strategy used when I discussed the "Sunday Special" in the chapter on recruiting techniques. If the applicant is in the personnel office, the questions can be asked within the context of a stand-up interview.

Critical, make-or-break questions are those directly related to the skills and characteristics needed for successful performance on the job. The following questions may serve as useful examples:

1. How fast can you type (or take stenography)?
2. To what tolerances can you work (asked of a tool and die maker)?
3. What type of consumer goods sales experience have you had?
4. What are your salary requirements?
5. Can you work on weekends (nights)?
6. Are you willing to work shift hours?
7. Do you have an automobile available for work?
8. Are you available for travel up to 50 per cent of the time?
9. Do you have an accounting degree?
10. Are you a registered nurse in this state?

The answers, as they relate to the precise specifications developed for the position (see the chapter on Step 1), can help us determine whether to give the applicant further consideration.

Reviewing the Application Form

Reviewing the candidate's application form can often give us some indication of whether or not a more detailed and comprehensive interview is called for. A properly designed application form is an indispensable tool if we are going to develop and maintain a viable and effective staffing system. The candidate should be asked to complete an application relatively early in the employment process. As we shall see, it is unwise to conduct the structured selection interview with someone using only his own résumé, without the company's employment application. An applicant's résumé will tell us only what he wants us to know, not necessarily what we need to know.

Some borderline and totally incompetent applicants engage the services of so-called "employment consultants" to help them design elaborate, attractive résumés that extol their alleged virtues and abilities. These résumés are little more than tributes to the writing skills of the people preparing them. They often intentionally leave out highly valuable data, such as precise dates of employment. They may hide the fact that the applicant has had an erratic and choppy work record; that he has been out of work for an extended period of time; or that he has held one or more short-lived positions he would rather not have mentioned.

Figure 6 is an employment application my firm developed that is compatible with all equal employment opportunity requirements and guidelines. Note that the information asked for on the application form is completely job related and necessary for an objective evaluation of the candidate's qualifications. No irrelevant or unnecessary information—information that conceivably could be challenged as a violation of an EEO regulation—is requested.

Many danger signals can be spotlighted by a brief review of the application form. Some of the more common ones are:

1. Has the applicant a sketchy and erratic job history, with many brief periods of employment?
2. Are there time gaps in his employment record during which he apparently did not work?
3. Are there indications that because of his past compensation, his salary requirements will be higher than the figure the company is prepared to offer?
4. Has the applicant moved frequently from one part of the country to another, or from one type of work to another, suggesting a lack of personal stability or maturity?
5. Are his past experience and education related to our job specifications?

6. Do his reasons for having left previous positions suggest that he may be an undesirable or troublesome employee? For example, has he resigned from former positions because there was a "personality incompatibility," he "did not like superior," or "we agreed to disagree"?
7. Does the applicant possess any physical disability or health problem that would prevent him from carrying out the job?

A brief look at the employment application can suggest that no more time need be spent with the applicant. If the job seeker is on the premises, a "stand-up" interview can be administered to verify the impression given by the application. Should the candidate still appear to be unsuitable, he can be sent on his way. If the interviewer is satisfied with the candidate's responses, arrangements can be made for a subsequent more detailed interview.

Sometimes this type of applicant screening can be conducted over the telephone. A company may place a newspaper advertisement for a given position in a distant city. Before he is ready to have the applicant travel to the company's main offices or send a representative to the distant city, it might be wise for the personnel specialist to ask certain critical questions by telephone to determine whether the anticipated interview expenses are warranted.

Briefly Describing the Job to the Applicant

Another good way to eliminate unqualified applicants is to describe the job briefly to the candidate. Many applicants are completely unfamiliar with the requirements and duties of the job for which they are applying or with various related conditions of employment. For example, some jobs require work at night or on weekends. A willingness to accept shift assignments may be a condition of employment. Or the compensation offered may be much less than the individual is prepared to accept. Briefly describing

Figure 6. Application for employment, front.
The reverse side of the form is on the facing page.

APPLICATION FOR EMPLOYMENT

DATE _____

NAME (print) _____

TELEPHONE Home: _____
Office: _____

ADDRESS _____
STREET   CITY   STATE   ZIP CODE

POSITION DESIRED_____ SALARY EXPECTED $ _____

DATE OF BIRTH_____ 19 _____ U.S. CITIZEN ☐ YES ☐ NO
(Federal Law Prohibits Discrimination Based on Age)

PHYSICAL LIMITATIONS ☐ YES ☐ NO

EDUCATION

Type of School	Name of School	Location of School	Major Subject	Graduate?	Last Year Attended
HIGH SCHOOL					
COLLEGE					
GRADUATE SCHOOL					

LIST ANY ADDITIONAL SKILLS, KNOWLEDGE, EXPERIENCE OR OTHER RELEVANT QUALIFICATIONS:

_____
_____
_____
_____
_____
_____
_____
_____

(OVER)

WORK EXPERIENCE
(Including U.S. Military Service, If Any)*

List names & addresses of all former employers beginning with the most recent.	Nature of Business	Dates of Employment				Position	Starting Salary	Final Salary	Reason for Leaving	Name of Superior
		From		To						
		Mo.	Yr.	Mo.	Yr.					
1										Name / Title
2										Name / Title
3										Name / Title
4										Name / Title
5										Name / Title

INDICATE BY NUMBER _____ WHICH EMPLOYERS YOU DO NOT WISH US TO CONTACT.

As part of our employment process, an investigation may be made with respect to an applicant's credit status, character, general reputation, personal characteristics and mode of living. Additional information as to the nature and scope of such a report, if made, will be provided upon the written request of the applicant.

Date _____ 19 _____ Signature _____

*Do not ask in New Jersey

some of the key aspects of the job—possibly within the framework of a stand-up mini interview—can save the personnel practitioner a lot of time. Numerous applicants will find the conditions of employment as described to be unacceptable, and will remove themselves voluntarily from any further consideration.

I can give a personal example of how, by merely describing the job to a group of unqualified applicants, the screening process can be facilitated. The company I worked for maintained an elaborate training program to prepare people for a sales career. Attractively designed ads were frequently run in *The New York Times* inviting interested candidates to apply to the personnel department. Because of the company's reputation and prominence in the industry, many people with extensive sales experience behind them would apply.

The company felt confident, however, that once the overqualified applicants were given some basic facts about the position, they would lose interest in the job. Consequently, whenever one or more experienced applicants would present themselves in the personnel department—stand-up interviews were sometimes conducted with several people simultaneously in order to conserve time—we would briefly describe the job, the relatively modest trainee salary that was offered, and the unavoidably mundane and fairly junior tasks that were traditionally performed by beginners embarking on a sales career. Invariably, these seasoned and experienced candidates would indicate that they could not see themselves starting over again in a junior capacity. Obviously, a long and extensive interview with such people would have been a complete waste of time on both sides.

Which technique, or combination of techniques, to use in screening out applicants depends on individual circumstances. Experimenting a bit with the different methods is likely to expedite the departure of unqualified applicants and save the personnel professional a good deal of valuable time.

PSYCHOLOGICAL EVALUATION TECHNIQUES AND PERSONNEL SELECTION

Professional industrial psychologists have made significant contributions to the field of personnel selection. Psychological tests have been developed and introduced in a large number of companies to assist them in selecting better applicants. A fairly large number of professionally developed psychological tests are now available to measure such factors as intelligence, specific abilities and aptitudes, motor dexterity, occupational interests, and personality variables.

Moreover, well-established firms of industrial psychologists all over the United States are prepared to assist organizations in selecting managerial and executive personnel by conducting individual psychological evaluations of candidates being considered for employment or promotion. Such psychological evaluations should be conducted only by thoroughly experienced industrial psychologists holding a doctorate degree and having extensive practical experience in business and industry. They should consist of an intensive and in-depth interview with the psychologist, supplemented by appropriately selected tests measuring various intellectual and personality factors. Appendix B is an example of a typical psychological evaluation conducted on behalf of an executive applicant.

PSYCHOLOGICAL TESTING AND EQUAL EMPLOYMENT OPPORTUNITY

Many companies have used psychological tests within their personnel departments for years in selecting and placing applicants for employment. However, stringent enforcement of equal employment opportunity guidelines by various government agencies has caused some of these companies to decide to stop this practice completely. They took this action even though Title VII of the Civil Rights Act of 1964 specifically permits—even encourages—companies to use professionally developed psychological selection techniques.

Interestingly, in passing the Civil Rights Act of 1964, Congress intended to facilitate, not inhibit, the use of professional psychological selection methods through the so-called Tower Amendment (proposed by Senator John Tower, Rep., Texas). This amendment states ". . . nor shall it be an unlawful employment practice for an employer to give and to act upon the results of any professionally developed ability test . . ." (Section 703).

Moreover, the much-publicized Guidelines on Employee Selection Procedures issued by the Equal Employment Opportunity Commission (EEOC) recognize the advantages of properly developed and used psychological selection techniques. Section 1607.1 clearly says that ". . . it is also recognized that professionally developed tests, when used in conjunction with other tools of personnel assessment and complemented by sound programs of job design, may significantly aid in the development and maintenance of an efficient work force and, indeed, aid in the utilization and conservation of human resources generally."

Nevertheless, even though the law permits companies to use psychological tests in personnel selection and placement, in actual practice stringent and often highly impractical requirements insisted on by the EEOC and other government agencies to furnish virtually indisputable validation evidence that the test used is, in fact, a valid predictor of subsequent on-the-job performance has posed an almost insurmountable obstacle. It is true that quite a number of companies have launched extensive research studies and have succeeded in validating their testing programs. As a result, they have had their personnel selection systems approved and accepted by government regulatory agencies. But many more organizations have come to the conclusion that the cost, effort, and time needed to satisfy compliance agencies were not worth it and have decided to eliminate the use of psychological tests entirely.

Sometimes such a decision was justified, in other cases it was unwise. Even though test validation is often complex and time consuming, it need not be so in every instance. In view of the many legal–psychometric issues surrounding the use of psychological tests in personnel selection, I suggest that a company intending to use this technique seek the assistance of a qualified and competent consulting industrial psychologist thoroughly familiar with all phases of the field.

USING SKILL AND ABILITY TESTS
TO SCREEN OUT THE UNQUALIFIED

All we have said in the above section does not pertain to a company giving appropriate *skill* and *ability* tests to determine whether a job applicant has the basic competence to perform the duties of the position for which he or she is applying. We are referring to such office positions as secretary, typist, and keypunch, switchboard, and teletype operators; such industrial positions as machinist and tool and die maker; and such technical positions as x-ray technician, drafting assistant, and computer programmer. According to the latest government guidelines, these ability or skill tests need not even be validated to satisfy compliance officers. So long as an objective content-focused job analysis will substantiate that a given and realistic degree of skill—a typing skill of 50 words per minute, for example—is necessary for the successful performance of the job, a company need have no concern in using a skill or ability test in personnel selection.

Indeed, I feel that it is imperative, as part of initial applicant screening, to verify the essential job skill the candidate lays claim to. There is no need to go any further in considering a secretary for employment if we find out—her claims of proficiency notwithstanding—that she cannot take shorthand well enough to satisfy the correspondence requirements of a busy sales manager. Such unqualified applicants should be screened out promptly.

DOCUMENTATION REQUIREMENTS
FOR EQUAL EMPLOYMENT
OPPORTUNITY PURPOSES

As I indicated in the second chapter, the government requires that accurate and complete records be obtained and kept for a period of at least one year on each and every job applicant who establishes a face-to-face contact with the company. More significantly, information must be gathered and maintained on the following eight factors:

1. Date of application
2. Name of applicant
3. Specific minority group of which applicant is a member
4. Sex
5. Position applied for
6. Appropriate equal employment opportunity classification category
7. Disposition of application for employment
8. Specific recruiting source that referred the applicant

I want to stress that these data must be recorded and retained for possible inspection by a government compliance officer for each person who has applied in person to the company. (The regulation does not ordinarily pertain to the person who merely telephoned the company to determine whether any jobs were available or wrote in asking about employment.) Furthermore, you should be cautioned to be quite specific and detailed with regard to the disposition of the application in recording the reason for the applicant's rejection. If you keep records properly, you will be fully prepared to justify your decision if a discrimination charge is filed against the company by a job applicant. As an illustration, stating on the application that the candidate had a poor appearance is not enough. A more detailed notation, saying that the applicant appeared unshaven and wore dirty or soiled clothes, would be much more defensible.

six

Step 4—Checking the applicant's employment references

ONCE WE HAVE reduced our original and relatively un-screened pool of job applicants through the initial screening process and given any pertinent skill or ability tests, we are ready for the next step in the Sequential Selection System: checking the applicant's previous employment references. The importance of a thorough check of the applicant's prior work experience cannot be emphasized enough. It is an indispensable part of effective personnel selection.

Unfortunately, many personnel specialists are reluctant to put in the time and effort needed to check an applicant's prior work record properly. A self-imposed defeatist attitude on the part of the personnel specialist himself may cause him to feel that he probably would not get an honest, thorough, and accurate response from the candidate's past employers anyway. As a result, he forgoes running a reference check. I regard this as an unfortunate decision. My experience has been that more often than not, the time and effort put into reference checking pays big dividends. The personnel professional often gains highly valuable and useful information related to the applicant's past work experience.

It would be an ideal world if every applicant's story were completely accurate. Unfortunately, in real life this is rarely the case. Many times they realize that to obtain employment, they will have to embellish their qualifications and try their best to hide their deficiencies and limitations from a discerning interviewer. Accordingly, some applicants will overstate their qualifications or achievements; others may be quite evasive and even untruthful; yet others may try to hide negative information from the interviewer.

Undisclosed information may consist of one or more former positions the applicant has held but would prefer not to mention. Or the applicant may have been discharged from a previous job, for reasons that would damage his chances for a new job. He may have a serious and disqualifying health or physical disability he will try to hide from the interviewer.

In short, the job seeker knows that if he is to make a favorable impression on the personnel specialist, he will need to put his best foot forward. Therefore, his strategy may be to overstate his qualifications or give false information. Or he may intentionally omit information of a highly critical nature. Therefore, it is of the utmost importance that the applicant's prior employment references be thoroughly checked.

METHODS OF CHECKING REFERENCES

A number of methods have been used over the years to check employment references. Predominantly they fall into three categories: checking references in person, by mail, and by telephone. We shall discuss each technique in this chapter.

In Person

Probably the best single way of checking an applicant's reference is to pay a personal visit to his former employer. I do not recommend this technique when filling lower-level jobs, primarily because of the extra time and expense this method requires. It is useful, however, in checking references of candidates for more responsible managerial and executive positions. In a person-to-person interview, you can usually extract considerably more valuable and indepth information than you can from any other method.

Moreover, a former employer is sometimes impressed and even flattered by the extra effort shown in seeking him out for a recommendation. As a result, he is more disposed to elaborate on his former employee's qualifications and experience. Both as a personnel executive and currently as an executive recruiter, I have gone out into the field to conduct in-person reference checks and been most gratified with the wealth of information generated.

By Mail

The most popular method of checking an applicant's employment references is by sending a letter to his former company. I do not recommend this technique. To begin with, sending a reference letter is ordinarily a long and drawn-out procedure. By the time the answer comes, one to two weeks may easily have elapsed. By that time the applicant may have become tired of waiting for the company's answer and accepted employment elsewhere. Also, companies are increasingly wary and reluctant to put any meaningful information down on paper because of a concern—statistically rare as it may be—that they might be challenged by their former employee to justify or defend their comments. Therefore, many companies will only verify dates of employment and job titles of their former employees—not very meaningful information on which to base a hiring decision.

By Telephone

Using the telephone to check references is, in my opinion, the most useful strategy to employ. Consequently, most of the rest of this chapter will be devoted to this particular technique. Telephone reference checking has numerous practical advantages. It is an immediate method of obtaining reference information; it often provides the interviewer with a considerable amount of useful knowledge about the applicant; it is a relatively inexpensive way to generate information; and it may suggest important additional areas of inquiry regarding the candidate's background and qualifications that warrant further exploration during the course of the subsequent interview.

Less Useful Techniques

Other, far less useful methods of checking references have been used. Before we concentrate on the telephone approach, I will discuss these less desirable techniques briefly. Some companies still put stock in "To whom it may concern" or similar reference letters voluntarily shown to the interviewer by the applicant. Usually these letters are laudatory and very general and therefore provide very little, if any, useful or analytical information. In some instances such letters have actually been written on company stationery by the applicant himself, or by a friend requested to make favorable statements on behalf of the candidate.

Surprising as it may be, some companies still request personal references from the job applicant. In our experience, this is utterly worthless. Just about everybody has a friend, neighbor, or relative who is prepared to say good things about him. Another useless technique is requesting reference information from prominent or prestigious members of the applicant's home community. The applicant's physician, dentist, or clergyman (in view of recent court decisions, this last category is almost certainly a violation of equal employment opportunity regulations and might result in a discrimination charge) rarely has any direct, firsthand, or work-related knowledge about the applicant. Asking questions of the candidate's former teachers or professors is also not likely to be very helpful. These people, like those mentioned above, customarily have only a superficial knowledge of the applicant.

THE TELEPHONE REFERENCE CHECK

In conducting the telephone reference check, who should you contact to obtain the needed information? Without any question, the person you need to talk to is the applicant's immediate superior. Some personnel people erroneously believe that they should speak with their counterpart in the personnel department. This is almost always a mistake. The personnel department will only have indirect information. Usually only the candidate's direct superior has the full array of qualitative information needed. If, when calling the applicant's former company, you learn that the candidate's superior has himself moved on to another company, find out where he has gone and promptly telephone him at his new place of business.

Check Before the Structured Selection Interview

You may already have asked yourself why reference checking should *precede* the Structured Selection Interview. You might even wonder if it would not be more logical to interview the applicant first and verify the information obtained during the course of the interview later.

Actually, some measure of flexibility may be introduced at this point. For example, if you are considering a person for a higher level position and have a good deal of confidence that the recruiting source (for example, a competent employment agency or an executive search firm) has done an effective job of prescreening, you might prefer to conduct the reference check *after* interviewing the candidate. This strategy may be particularly appropriate if you plan to conduct a second in-depth interview with the applicant before a final decision is made.

On the other hand, the advantages of conducting the telephone reference check before the interview may be great, particularly when there has been no prescreening. A review of the candidate's application form may raise a specific question regarding his basic qualifications, suggesting that a full Structured Selection Interview is not warranted. For example, suppose a job seeker has given nebulous reasons for leaving his last job, such as "wanted more advancement," "did not like my supervisor," or "disagreed with company policy." It might be a good idea to run a telephone reference check before investing the time necessary to conduct a full Structured Selection Interview. The facts supplied by the applicant's former superior may be so negative as to preclude his employment. Spending a few minutes on the telephone has saved the time and bother of a fruitless comprehensive interview. In essence, then, a telephone check before the interview can serve as yet another strategic screening-out step in our Sequential Selection System.

In addition, the information obtained during the course of the telephone reference check may provide useful cues as to what to ask or look for during the interview. If a former superior tells us that the applicant was generally satisfactory but sometimes displayed a degree of immaturity or carelessness in his work, we are forearmed with this information and can make this area one of special inquiry during the course of the interview.

How to Conduct the Check

Let us examine in detail how we can best obtain information regarding the applicant's background on the telephone. The personnel specialist should place the call directly to the applicant's former superior, identifying himself, his position, and the name of his organization. I strongly recommend the use of the telephone reference check form that appears as Figure 7. It was specifically designed to facilitate the gathering of the proper information. Note that this is a *structured* and *sequential* reference form. The questions the personnel interviewer should ask appear on the left-hand side, with space for the respondent's answers provided on the right-hand side of the form.

There are many advantages to working from a prepared and structured telephone reference check. The main one is that it enables the personnel practitioner to conduct an efficient, fast, and continuous interview with the applicant's former boss. And because the personnel specialist has the key critical questions he should ask right at his fingertips, he is more likely to get accurate and truthful answers. He is asking all the important questions in rapid and sequential order—a strategy that almost always results in getting the facts, primarily because the technique does not give the respondent sufficient time to contrive or fabricate answers, even if he is disposed to do so.

Starting the telephone reference check with item 1 on the form, "I would like to verify some of the information given to us by Mr. _____," usually gets the interview right off the ground. It signifies to the respondent that the caller already has certain facts, and that he merely wants to verify or confirm the information he has. The telephone check is now launched. With proper continuity, it facilitates obtaining additional and much more comprehensive reference information.

Although it is suggested that the questions be asked in the order in which they appear on the form, the user should be relatively flexible in his approach. He should bear in mind that the telephone reference check is really an interview. As such, it requires a certain degree of adaptability on the part of the interviewer. For example, here and there he may wish to ask a question that does not appear on the form

Figure 7. Telephone reference check form.

NAME OF APPLICANT _____

PERSON CONTACTED _____ POSITION OR TITLE _____

COMPANY _____ CITY & STATE _____ TEL. NO. _____

1. I would like to verify some of the information given to us by (Mr., Miss, Mrs.) _____
who is applying for a position with our company. What were the dates of his (her) employment with you?

   From _____ 19____ To _____ 19____

2. What was the nature of his (her) job? _____

3. What did you think of his (her) work? _____

4. How would you describe his (her) performance in comparison with other people? _____

5. What job progress did he (she) make? _____

6. What were his (her) earnings? _____

7. Why did he (she) leave your company? _____

8. Would you re-employ? ☐ Yes ☐ No (Why not) _____

9. What are his (her) strong points?

_____

10. What are his (her) limitations?

_____

11. How did he (she) get along with other people?

_____

12. Could you comment on his (her)
    (a)   attendance
    (b)   dependability
    (c)   ability to take on responsibility
    (d)   potential for advancement
    (e)   degree of supervision needed
    (f)   overall attitude

_____

13. Did he (she) have any personal difficulties that interfered
    with his (her) work?

_____

14. Is there anything else of significance that we should know?

_____

_____   _____
DATE   19   CHECKED BY

in order to obtain further elaboration or clarification of a statement made by the respondent.

Overcoming Resistance

At this point, you may be saying, "Okay, it sounds easy. But what if the person you are calling says that it is against company policy to give reference information over the telephone and he does not want to talk to you?" Admittedly, this can be a real problem, and it is becoming more commonplace. Nevertheless, the problem can be overcome without any unusual difficulty if you use some of the helpful hints supplied below.

To begin with, the personnel practitioner must be convinced in his own mind that he needs this information to make a fair, accurate, and objective hiring decision, and that he has every right to it. Consequently, he should feel no reluctance or compunction whatever in asking for that information. If he is confident and persistent in his approach, he should be successful in overcoming resistance to providing the needed information. He should, of course, stress that everything he hears will be held in confidence.

Let us take a closer look at precisely how such resistance can be overcome. If the respondent is unwilling to provide the information, the caller should be insistent, emphasizing that he needs the information now in order to give the applicant fair consideration. As an extra inducement, he might mention that if he cannot verify the applicant's information, the candidate may be excluded from further consideration for the job. This tactic frequently motivates the respondent to provide the needed information.

If the respondent still insists that it is against company policy to furnish such information over the telephone, the interviewer should state that he appreciates the company's policy, but ask if an exception could not be made in this instance. If the candidate's former boss continues to balk, the personnel specialist should ask to speak to someone at the next higher level of management. This strategy more often than not resolves the difficulty.

Additional Aids

The astute personnel professional should be particularly sensitive to *how* the respondent talks about his former employee. Does he speak positively, enthusiastically, or even glowingly of the applicant, or is he curt, brief, and relatively guarded in his comments? We have already pointed out that the telephone reference check should be regarded in the same light as an interview. The personnel practitioner must be perceptive and skilled in conducting this type of interview so that he can interpret the information he gets correctly. A great deal can be learned about the applicant by listening carefully not only to *what* the candidate's former boss says about him but *how* he says it.

Some people are by nature placid, nonenthusiastic, or excessively critical, and would not be very positive about anyone or anything. Therefore, the personnel specialist must give some consideration to the nature and personality of the reference giver as well as to what is said if he is going to come up with a true and correct understanding of the candidate's total qualifications.

A job applicant may not receive a favorable reference from one employer. This should not mean that he should be automatically rejected. Failure in one position does not necessarily forecast failure in another assignment. A candidate may have had a personality clash with his former superior, but the fault may not have been his. You must check with more than one employer. In fact, every significant period of employment should be checked before a final evaluation of the applicant's qualifications is made.

Yet another situation warrants discussion. From time to time, it is imperative to check with an applicant's *present* employer. The job he has now may be the most relevant or the only significant employment he has had to date. Complicating this situation is the fact that the applicant will not permit a prospective new employer to check with his company if he fears jeopardizing his job. Yet what we would be buying in this instance, if we were to hire the applicant, is the precise experience he has gained in his present job. This makes it all the more necessary to check it out. Sometimes an indirect reference can be obtained (from a mutual vendor, supplier, or customer, or perhaps from a colleague of the applicant) without any risk to him. But in general, indirect references are not really satisfactory and should be avoided.

How, then, can this type of situation be handled? Somewhere in the interview—either within the context of the mini interview, or during the subsequent Structured Selection Interview—the applicant should be told that if he is given a firm offer of employment, it will be contingent upon receiving a satisfactory reference from his present company. The personnel practitioner should inform the candidate that once he has been given a definite offer, he will be expected to resign from his job. At that point the candidate's employer will be called for a reference. If it is not completely satisfactory, the company reserves the right to withdraw the offer. This strategy usually has the beneficial effect of making the candidate truthful in stating his qualifications. Moreover, the company will be able to withdraw its offer gracefully in the unlikely event that circumstances warrant such an action.

Compliance with the Fair Credit Reporting Act

In the past, many companies routinely secured investigative reports, or so-called "neighborhood checks," to obtain additional information regarding an applicant's financial reliability, character, and mode of living and to determine the possible existence of a criminal record. These reports are available throughout the country from both national and local credit reporting services. They were used frequently by companies considering applicants for positions in which they would have access to money. In 1971, however, the Fair Credit Reporting Act became effective. Because of some of its provisions, it has had the effect of significantly reducing the use of such reports.

Because of special circumstances, some companies still find these "consumer investigative reports" of value in their personnel selection, and continue to use them. However, an organization intending to utilize them should bear in mind that the Fair Credit Reporting Act requires certain steps to be taken in accordance with the law.

To begin with, companies planning to obtain such reports are legally obligated to inform the applicant that an investigation may be conducted. For this reason it is suggested that as part of the company's application form (see the preceding chapter), the following statement be included, and that the applicant be asked to sign the form indicating that he has read it: "As part of our employment process, an investigation may be made with respect to an applicant's credit status, character, general reputation, personal characteristics, and mode of living. Additional information as to the nature and scope of such a report, if made, will be provided upon the written request of the applicant."

The consumer reporting agency conducting the investigation must also notify the applicant that the company has requested a report and inform the candidate that he may review the information that has been obtained about him. Under the law, if a company denies employment to an applicant wholly or partly because of information contained in a consumer report, they must advise him accordingly and give him the name and address of the agency that made the report. If the applicant finds that the information contained in his file is erroneous, he has the right to submit his own explanation of the facts in question. This must then be summarized by the reporting agency and sent to the prospective employer. In any case, the company retains the right to decide which version of the story it wishes to accept—that of the reporting agency or that of the applicant.

seven

Psychological insights in selecting personnel

BEFORE WE CAN DISCUSS the mechanics of the Structured Selection Interview, we must become familiar with certain psychological insights. To conduct an employment interview, we must possess a degree of knowledge and understanding of the principles of the behavior and motivation of people at work. This knowledge is extremely important if we are going to make accurate predictions of which applicants are likely to make a useful contribution to our company and which are likely to fail.

It is not difficult to select appropriate questions to ask the applicant in an employment interview. You probably have certain favorites you feel have served you well in the past and plan to use them again. My own list of Tested

Questions, which appears in Appendix A, contains numerous inquiries intended to provide the astute interviewer with a wealth of comprehensive and in-depth information about the applicant in order to arrive at an accurate prediction of probably future job success.

The problem is not which questions to ask. What is a lot harder is to *interpret* the information given to us by the job seeker correctly. The personnel professional needs a conceptual model—a practical frame of reference—on which to base his overall conclusions once he has obtained all the pertinent information about the applicant.

Conceptual Foundation of the Structured Selection Interview

Ever since the first employer went out to hire someone to work for him, countless theories have been offered to help predict future on-the-job performance. While some of these theories have been based on some frail scientific premise, most of them were predicated on no more than the highly personal and numerically limited anecdotal experience of its advocate.

With the exception of the conceptual model offered below, not a single scientific hypothesis or theory related to performance prediction has consistently withstood the test of empirical and investigative scrutiny. What frame of reference, then, can assist the personnel professional in making a more accurate prediction of probable future job success? I believe that the following principle will serve as a most useful guide in personnel selection.

Future Prediction Based on Past Performance

Of all the theories that have been offered to assist employers in making better hiring decisions, only one is really practical. This theory states that the best way to predict an applicant's future job performance is to take a good look at what he or she has done in the past. A clear understanding of what a person has done is the single best way to predict his future behavior. This explanation of human behavior is based on the fact that an individual's basic personality, attitudes, motivation, and behavior pattern tend to be established fairly early in life—often during childhood and adolescence—and, as a rule, are quite resistant to change. Accordingly, human behavior has a strong tendency to follow along the same continuum, rather than to change direction drastically.

Applying this behavior theory to the field of employment, it follows that if a particular job applicant has had a good record in school, has had a stable and continuous history of employment, and has been successful and productive in former positions, he is unlikely to depart from such a behavior profile and develop a negative pattern of employment. Similarly, an applicant who has had a fairly consistent record of unsatisfactory and unsuccessful employment is likely to follow along this continuum, and will probably not alter his behavior so dramatically as to become a notably productive employee.

Of course, exceptions do occur. No doubt you can remember a particular case of a successful person who underwent a radical behavior change for the worse; or of a so-called "late bloomer" who, after many initial failures in his career, finally "straightened himself out" and went on to success. Recognizing the wide variability in human behavior, such situations are bound to occur. But despite the human interest aspect of these exceptions, statistically speaking they are rare and should not be counted on in practicing the art and science of personnel selection.

There is an important corollary to the theory I have just proposed. I shall discuss this next.

Assessment of the Applicant's Total Behavior Profile

A comprehensive interview should generate both positive and negative items of input. It is unusual not to uncover *some* negative information that will detract—if ever so slightly—from an otherwise positive total profile. Similarly, an unqualified applicant will generally reveal several positive items of information regarding his background. You must be sure that you are evaluating the applicant's *overall* and *total* behavior profile in order to determine his *usual* and *typical* behavior response.

Exceptions to the candidate's overall behavior profile must be recognized for what they are and should not overly influence your total assessment of his qualifications. The Structured Selection Interview, to be discussed in Chapter 8, is designed to enable the personnel professional to arrive at an accurate assessment of the applicant's overall behavior profile.

Interviewing from the Head, Not the Heart

Most personnel practitioners have a high inherent degree of humanism and sensitivity toward people. This sensitivity probably influenced their decision to seek a career in the field of human resource administration. However, to be a truly professional employment specialist, a person must learn to maintain an objective, analytical, and critical posture in evaluating an applicant and to interview that applicant with his head and not his heart. You must constantly bear in mind that your primary responsibility in personnel selection is to the organization and your chief task is to recruit and hire the best possible person for the job—one who will make a worthwhile contribution to the company.

Complicating the personnel professional's job is that quite regularly the unsatisfactory applicant will arrive at the interview exceedingly well prepared and possibly even skillfully rehearsed. He knows his shortcomings and the deficiencies in his employment history. He knows he must make the company disregard any limitations or disqualifications it may uncover in his employment record.

It is not unusual for the marginal or borderline applicant

to have a well-perfected set of alibis, excuses, and rationalizations to explain away an unsatisfactory record. Some applicants may even have secured the assistance of so-called
"job consulting services" that help them go through a series
of simulated role-playing interviewing sessions intended to
prepare them to field the personnel interviewer's probing
questions adroitly and to give favorable but contrived and
false responses.

The personnel professional, however, must develop and
maintain an analytical, probing, and critical posture. He
must discount the applicant's rationalization that the past is
all behind him, his explanation that what he has done before bears no relation to the future, and his promise to turn
over a new leaf. The well-prepared and well-rehearsed job
seeker is likely to sound very sincere and convincing. The
ease with which he tells his story probably indicates that he
has gained a good deal of experience in telling it, and that it
gets better with each telling. All such rationalizations and
promises—well-intentioned though they may be—must be
disregarded by the interviewer. The personnel professional
must remember that he cannot afford to fall prey to senti-
mentality and emotion.

At the same time, for public relations considerations, the
interviewer must not let the applicant feel any criticism or
disapproval of what he has done in the past. The interviewer's interpretations, conclusions, and final assessment
are his own and should be kept to himself. They should not
be reflected or revealed inadvertently to the applicant. One
of the hallmarks of the truly professional interviewer is the
ability to conduct a skillful interview without in any way
revealing his overall assessment of the candidate's qualifications.

Evaluating the Applicant's Qualifications

In interviewing a job candidate, precisely what information
should we look for? Which abilities, skills, traits, and

characteristics should be taken into account? Which qualifications are relevant in determining whether or not to make a concrete job offer to the applicant? It is probably impossible to come up with a total, all-encompassing list of qualifications that will cover every conceivable job. In fact, most positions have their own very definite set of specifications.

Nevertheless, I will attempt to offer a fairly comprehensive set of qualifications that serve as a useful frame of reference against which to gauge and evaluate the information obtained from the applicant. For each particular position we try to fill, however, we must be careful to select and evaluate only those specifications that have a direct bearing. In order to satisfy equal employment opportunity requirements, we must be certain that the qualifications we are trying to evaluate in the applicant are both job related and necessary for the assignment in question.

The strategy we will employ to evaluate the job seeker's qualifications will be to use the Tested Questions for the Structured Selection Interview (see Appendix A). The questions should bring out the background information needed to arrive at an ultimate selection decision. The strategy is based on the idea that what the candidate has done in the past is the best indication of what he will do for us if he joins our organization. For the sake of convenience, the list of qualifications will be divided into three categories. An understanding of what the applicant has done with relation to these qualifications will help us to predict what he will do. The qualifications, placed in their appropriate categories, are:

BASIC ABILITIES

Intelligence and mental alertness
Job knowledge and skills
Education
Experience

Organizational skills
Communication skills
Energy level

PERSONAL CHARACTERISTICS

Interpersonal skills (poise and bearing)
Manner and attitude
Interpersonal assertiveness
Initiative, drive, and resourcefulness
Maturity
Motivation and ambition

CHARACTER TRAITS

Stability
Industry
Perseverance
Ability to get along with others
Confidence and self-reliance
Leadership

Now that we have identified the qualifications we want to assess, let us see precisely how we can interpret and evaluate the information given to us by the applicant. The rest of this chapter is devoted to a rather detailed itemization of all the questions you must keep in mind as part of the evaluation process for each of the qualifications listed above.

BASIC ABILITIES

Intelligence and Mental Alertness
- How mentally alert and responsive is the applicant?
- How well does he follow your train of thought during the interview?
- How well has the candidate done academically while in high school and college?

- Is he able to draw the proper inferences and conclusions during the course of the interview?
- Does the applicant demonstrate a degree of intellectual depth in his conversation, or does he appear to be shallow and superficial in his thinking?
- Has he used good judgment and common sense in the way he has planned and led his life so far?
- Does he appear to be able to think and to respond spontaneously?
- What is the applicant's capacity for problem-solving activities?

Job Knowledge and Skills
- Does the applicant possess the necessary skill level and knowledge to handle the assignment?
- To what extent is he aware of anticipated changes and developments in his particular field?

Education
- Does the applicant possess the basic educational background to qualify for the job?

Experience
- Has the applicant had sufficient experience to qualify for the position in question?
- Has the applicant had a successful record of accomplishments in the jobs he previously held, or is his record relatively lackluster and without any true distinction?
- Has the applicant progressed in his career, proceeding from less responsible assignments to positions of increasing scope, complexity, and magnitude?
- Has his compensation increased to reflect his achievements and contribution to his employer, or have his salary increases been relatively modest and perhaps little more than enough to keep up with inflation?

Organizational Skills
- How skilled has the applicant been in planning, organizing, and controlling his work?
- Does the applicant appear to have a systematic and logical approach to work?
- Is he able to keep his priorities in order, or does he lose sight of the really important matters?

Communication Skills
- How verbal and articulate is the applicant?
- Is he able to make an effective presentation and to sell his ideas to others?
- Are his thoughts, ideas, and points of view expressed in a believable, persuasive, and convincing manner?
- Is the applicant skilled at overcoming the objections of others?
- Is he able to influence the behavior and thinking of people with whom he comes into contact?

Energy Level
- What is the applicant's energy level? Has he generally been active?
- Does his past history reveal a record of having been engaged in many different and productive activities?
- While in school and at college, did the applicant take part in many types of activities?

PERSONAL CHARACTERISTICS

Interpersonal Skills (poise and bearing)
- How effective is the applicant's overall presentation and impact upon others? What is the applicant's degree of poise and bearing?
- Does he project a degree of personal warmth in his interaction with others?
- Is he willing to cooperate and to collaborate with other people in order to achieve mutual goals?

- How tactful and diplomatic is he in interfacing with others?
- Does he reveal a degree of tact and social sensitivity in relating to other people?
- Is he excessively introverted and shy with other people, thus lessening his managerial or supervisory effectiveness?

Manner and Attitude

- Does the applicant have a positive manner and attitude in the way he presents himself?
- Is he exceedingly rigid, inflexible, or opinionated in his viewpoints and behavior?

Interpersonal Assertiveness

- Is the applicant assertive in the way he goes about attaining his own objectives?
- How competitive is the applicant?
- Has he allowed others to take undue advantage of him because of an absence of self-confidence or assertiveness?

Initiative, Drive, and Resourcefulness

- Does the applicant display initiative, drive, and resourcefulness, or is he the type of person who must be closely supervised and directed by his superiors?
- Has he demonstrated that he is a self-starter, or is he the type of person who needs to be prodded into action?
- Has he come up with new ideas or innovations in the past?

Maturity

- Does the applicant demonstrate a high degree of self-discipline, or is he overly pleasure oriented, preferring to avoid work and responsibility?
- Is the applicant a goal-directed individual who applies himself in a serious, conscientious, and purposive manner?

- What is the extent of the applicant's maturity and sense of responsibility?
- Does he appear to have a responsible and mature outlook on life?
- Does he appear to be self-directed and know where he wants to go, or are his plans completely indefinite and constantly subject to change?
- Is he excessively self-centered, or is he capable of identifying with his company's goals and objectives?
- How realistic and mature are his future plans and goals?
- How realistic are his salary expectations?
- Did he leave former jobs for reasonable, sound, and logical reasons?
- Does he appear to have a degree of insight into himself, or is he shallow and superficial?
- Has he been conscientious in the manner in which he has carried out past responsibilities?

Motivation and Ambition
- How ambitious and career oriented is the applicant?
- How high are his career aspirations?
- Has he taken any concrete steps to further his self-development?
- Has he an ongoing program to improve his skills and knowledge?
- Is he aware of his limitations and shortcomings, and is he doing something to attempt to overcome them?
- Is the applicant truly motivated toward the types of satisfactions likely to prevail in the position for which he is applying?

CHARACTER TRAITS

Stability
- Is the candidate a reasonably well-adjusted individual who has demonstrated a stable behavior pattern?

- How well does the candidate respond to stress and pressure?
- Has he remained in each job for a reasonable period of time, or has he jumped from one position to another frequently?
- Does there appear to be a degree of consistency in the type of employment he has held, or has he moved from one job to another in a haphazard manner?
- Is there a degree of permanence and stability in his pattern of interests, or does he flit from one avocational area to another?
- Does his job history indicate considerable erratic or short-term employment?
- Is he impulsive, frequently acting without carefully considering the effect of his actions?
- Is he able to maintain an even keel when facing problems or difficult situations, either of a work or a personal nature?

Perseverance
- Is the applicant persistent and persevering, or does he give up easily when encountering obstacles and difficulties?
- Has he stuck to difficult assignments, or was he inclined to quit at the first sign of difficulty?
- Has he finished what he started out to do with respect to his past education and employment?
- Has he always looked for the easy way out, or has he focused his abilities and energy toward seeing a difficult situation through to its final conclusion?

Industry
- In his work history, has the applicant been singled out for recognition, and has he received any particular awards, prizes, or distinction?
- Does he appear to have worked hard in his former jobs and did he make progress in them, or does the contrary appear to be true?

- Have there been extended periods of unemployment or inactivity in his work history?
- Has there been progress in his compensation?
- Has he advanced in his career, or has he remained stationary?
- Is he willing to work hard and to throw himself enthusiastically into the job?
- Does he identify with the company that employs him, or is he reluctant to make a commitment to the organization?
- Does he show evidence of sufficient self-discipline?
- Is he work and goal oriented, or primarily interested in leisure-time activities?
- Is he willing to extend himself on the job on behalf of his company?

Ability to Get Along with Others
- How effective is the candidate in dealing and working with others?
- Is he willing to accept advice, suggestions, and direction from superiors?
- What is the candidate's ability to function as a member of a team?
- Is he able to build and maintain effective relationships with other people?
- Has he frequently resigned from former jobs because of "personality incompatibility" or similar reasons?
- Does he take part in group activities, or does he follow more solitary interests?
- Does the applicant speak positively and favorably of past employers, professors, and teachers, or does he display a high degree of negativism in discussing his relationships with these people?
- Is the applicant highly critical of former superiors or of companies for which he has worked?
- Does he display a critical attitude in discussing

rules, regulations, and policies that existed in his former companies?

Confidence and Self-Reliance

- Does the candidate demonstrate the ability to function independently and without the need for close supervision, assistance, and direction?
- Is he able to respond to new situations in a flexible manner, or is he highly rigid and less able to adapt to new situations?
- Is the candidate able to work in a relatively ambiguous, uncertain, and unstructured work environment, or does he require an atmosphere that is highly planned and organized and not subject to unanticipated situations?
- Does the candidate reveal a high degree of confidence in himself?
- Is the applicant able to make a decision and live with it?
- Is the applicant self-reliant and able to stand on his own two feet?
- Has he been able to solve his own problems, or does he lean excessively on other people for support and direction?
- At what point did he become self-supporting?

Leadership

- Does the candidate appear to be able to motivate other people?
- Is the applicant able to gain the support, confidence, and following of other people?
- When the occasion requires, is he tough-minded enough and willing to take a definite stand on an issue?
- What is the candidate's potential for future growth and advancement?
- Has he been elected to any offices?

- In the past, has he been looked to by others for leadership, direction, and guidance?
- Has he had any supervisory responsibilities?
- Does his job record indicate that he has successfully held positions of increasingly greater scope and responsibility?
- To what extent has he accepted responsibility, and how successful has he been in these instances?
- If applying for a supervisory or managerial position, would he be able to direct the activities of subordinates effectively and maintain a high degree of departmental productivity?

eight

Step 5—The structured selection interview

B<small>Y FAR THE MOST</small> important step in the Sequential Selection System is the Structured Selection Interview. At the same time, it is also the most time-consuming step. Nevertheless, bear in mind that only applicants who have survived the preceding screening steps will go through the Structured Selection Interview. All other applicants who were found to be unqualified have already been eliminated from further consideration. Assuming that we have organized our staffing system properly, only a relatively small number of promising candidates should remain to receive our serious consideration.

HOW TO APPROACH THE INTERVIEW

Research has demonstrated that employment interviews vary tremendously, depending, among other factors, upon the type of job applicant being considered. Probably no two interviews are identical, partly because the approach and strategy followed by applicants themselves differ considerably. Some job seekers are open, candid, and forthright in discussing their background and qualifications. Others are evasive and even falsify aspects of their background, fabricating and embellishing upon their credentials as they go along. As noted in the preceding chapter, some applicants are quite glib and articulate. Their explanations seem logical and convincing, aided in part by their experience from previous interviews. As a result, their stories sound better and more plausible with each telling.

Applicants also vary in the skill with which they handle employment interviews. There is the relaxed, poised, and seemingly confident person who acts as if being interviewed for a job were second nature to him. This is often a well-rehearsed and carefully studied facade intended to deceive the interviewer.

At the other end of the spectrum is the nervous, tense, and visibly uncomfortable applicant who has a great deal of difficulty in settling down and in elaborating upon his qualifications. Such a candidate may fidget excessively in his seat, be subject to an occasional stammer or hesitation in his speech, and perspire unduly. He should not be dismissed out of hand, however. The astute interviewer will recognize the signs of initial nervousness and take the necessary steps to put the applicant at ease.

The otherwise competent applicant may be totally inexperienced in the logistics of job hunting, and understandably prone to a considerable degree of nervousness. He may not have much experience looking for employment or fielding job interviews because he held his last position for a long time. Consequently, looking for work is a strange, unfamiliar, and uncomfortable experience for him. Then again, articles in the popular press notwithstanding, many of the more desirable job applicants are strongly committed to the work ethic and feel embarrassed and awkward at being out of work, anticipating that they may shortly be "on the beach." These candidates might have weighty family and financial responsibilities, and the prospect of being unemployed could easily provoke a high degree of anxiety.

What approach should the interviewer take? It is essential that he establish rapport with the applicant and put him completely at ease. Only if the applicant is relaxed and in a comfortable, nonpressured, and nonstressful situation will we be able to get a true and accurate picture of what he is like and how he might perform on the job.

To get a true picture of the applicant, the interviewer should be sincere, warm, and friendly and accept the person for what he or she is. As the interview progresses, the personnel specialist will begin to form some preliminary opinions and tentative conclusions. He will make some definite value judgments on what the applicant has done or not done in the course of his career.

However, to maintain the professional decorum and atmosphere of the interview, these assessments should not be shared with the candidate. If the interview is to progress smoothly and to generate sufficient information about the applicant, the personnel specialist must be careful not to act or sound judgmental. To do so might destroy the rapport of the interview, antagonize the applicant, and turn the interview into a debating session—if not into an actual argument. The personnel professional's approach should be predominantly one of generating job-related information from the candidate. He should accept him without in any way revealing or projecting criticism or disapproval of the candidate's past actions or qualifications.

This does not mean, however, that the interviewer will accept at face value all the applicant's statements or claims of accomplishments. Far from it. As we shall see in the next chapter, once the information has been obtained, the interviewer will methodically review all the facts at his disposal. During the interview itself, his task is merely to elicit the information, keeping his opinions and value judgments to himself.

COMMON INTERVIEWING ERRORS

It may be helpful to explore some of the errors made not only by the inexperienced interviewer but also by the more seasoned personnel specialist who frequently follows a casual and unsystematic approach. Not until we are able to see our own mistakes will we really be able to develop the skill necessary to conduct the Structured Selection Interview.

A great deal of research has been conducted on the types of errors likely to be made in conducting employment interviews. Many years of practical experience in conducting employment interviews is no guarantee of success in developing this particular skill. Experienced interviewers commit many of the same errors the neophyte does. Faulty interviewing practices, through repetition, become firmly entrenched in the interviewer's style.

Aggravating this situation is the fact that most experienced interviewers believe themselves to be competent, and the less successful ones are not aware of the errors they commit. Consequently, they go on year after year repeating the same mistakes, in essence reinforcing faulty interviewing habits. Let us look at some of the more common errors associated with the casual, unplanned, and unsystematic type of employment interview. We want to be sure these errors do not inadvertently become a part of our own interviewing style.

Failure to Establish Rapport

Probably one of the most common errors that occurs is the inability of the interviewer to establish rapport with the candidate. The interview never gets off the ground. No substantive discussion is ever initiated or conducted and the entire interview flounders. As a result, no real information regarding the applicant or his qualifications is obtained. Several areas of inquiry regarding the candidate's background may be touched upon, but for the most part the interviewer merely reviews the data he already has available from the candidate's application form.

Both the interviewer and the applicant are frequently aware that rapport was never really established. The applicant may concede that he was courteously treated by the interviewer, but still be disappointed and frustrated because he knows that he was never able to tell his story or to present his qualifications adequately. He feels let down, knowing that he has lost the opportunity to be seriously considered for the position he wanted.

The interviewer also realizes that something went wrong. He may be aware that the applicant's credentials looked interesting—at least on the application form—and wonder why, at the actual interview, the candidate did not make a better impression and "come across." His failure to establish proper rapport has prevented a competent job applicant and a good company from getting together. Later in this chapter, we will see just how this interview flaw can be overcome.

Failure to Have a Strategy

Some interviewers do not have a strategy or a particular plan of action to follow during the course of the interview. Lacking a system they just hope for the best. What they obtain is considerably less than that. Sometimes they are not even aware of the type of information they need to elicit. They don't know what questions to ask.

Nevertheless, when an interviewer finds himself seated across the desk from the applicant, he knows that he must engage in some semblance of conversation. In his embarrassment and discomfort, he is likely to conduct the interview in a number of inappropriate and counterproductive ways. He may ask whatever questions happen to come to mind, dwelling at length on such irrelevant items as the candidate's hobbies, politics, weather, or sports.

In his desire to keep the interview going, the unprepared interviewer may even accidentally violate the equal employment opportunity regulations. One employment specialist inadvertently asked about the applicant's ethnic origin in a desperate effort to make conversation. Sometimes, also, not knowing what to ask, the interviewer permits the conversation to stop and lapse into silence. However, before too long, the silence becomes embarrassing and he resumes the conversation, again grasping at straws and talking about anything that comes to mind.

Briefness of the Interview

A common error in many interviews is to make the entire process too brief and too superficial. The result is that not enough meaningful information is gathered. When the interview is properly conducted, there is a direct relationship between its length and the amount of useful information obtained.

This is not to say that each and every interview must be lengthy. Some will require more time than others, depending upon such factors as the applicant's age, the extent of his past education and experience, and the level of the job for which he is applying. For example, thirty minutes is ordinarily enough time to interview an applicant for an entry or junior-level clerical position while one to two hours may easily be needed to evaluate a managerial candidate. However, if the interview is too short, only surface information will emerge and the personnel specialist will not be able to evaluate such vital factors as the applicant's attitude, maturity, and motivation.

I do not want to imply that the interview must be prolonged after the personnel specialist is convinced that the applicant is not qualified. There are times when the interviewer, and perhaps the applicant, realizes that the candidate and the position are not suited to each other. Under such circumstances, it would be pointless to continue the discussion. We shall see later in this chapter how the personnel professional can terminate the interview promptly but tactfully under those circumstances. But as long as the interviewer is interested in the candidate as a viable job applicant, he should continue the discussion until he has obtained all the information he needs.

Incorrect Interpretation

Interviews frequently fail because the information that has been obtained is incorrectly interpreted. The reasons may be subtle. To begin with, there might be a communications gap between the interviewer and the job applicant, causing the interviewer to draw the wrong conclusions from what he hears.

The candidate may say he wants to leave his job because he is having difficulty in establishing a satisfactory working relationship with his superior and feels it would ultimately affect his progress in the company. Such a response could be interpreted in a number of different ways. The interviewer might conclude that the applicant lacks the necessary interpersonal skills to relate satisfactorily to other people. Another explanation might be that it is the candidate's superior who is difficult to work with. Incorrect interpretations and conclusions are easily reached in casual and unsystematic interviews. The interviewer must delve deeply into the applicant's background to obtain enough information to substantiate his evaluation of the candidate's qualifications.

Subconsciously, the applicant may remind the interviewer of someone else. It may be an employee of the firm who triggers a specific reaction based on a previous experience. The interviewer attributes the characteristics of the employee—positive or negative—to the new job applicant, disregarding the fact that although there may be similarities in their background and qualifications, they are two very different people.

Unconscious Biases or Preferences

In discussing unconscious biases or preferences, I am not referring to the types of situations to which the equal employment opportunity laws and regulations address themselves. Rather, I have in mind a fixed, negative, virtually automatic rejection of certain background factors or characteristics of a given applicant. Or, on the other side of the coin, it may be a strong subjective preference for certain personal factors or characteristics that are completely unrelated to the job specifications.

For example, some people are automatically impressed by graduates from the so-called "ivy league" colleges. Others think highly of applicants who served as junior officers with the armed forces or played football in college. And some people think poorly of any graduate from universities or colleges they do not hold in high esteem. So the school he went to could unduly prejudice the evaluation of a candidate.

To some extent, the findings here parallel the much-researched halo effect—the tendency to allow one specific trait or characteristic to influence the overall evaluation of a candidate. Unconscious bias or preference is so prevalent in interviews because people disposed to making this type of error are not aware of the mistake they are making, and therefore do not guard against it. They will make the same mistake again and again. The personnel specialist must beware of falling into this kind of trap.

Excessive Talking

Another reason many interviews go wrong is that the interviewer has done most of the talking and consequently learned very little about the applicant. There is a right time for the personnel specialist to talk—when he is providing the job seeker with pertinent information about the position. However, there is also a time for the interviewer to listen carefully if he is going to obtain meaningful and relevant information. Too many interviewers do most of the talking and do not get more information about the candidate than the data already on the application form.

Sometimes the unskilled interviewer interrupts an applicant with a question or a comment, cutting off what might have been highly relevant new facts. As long as the applicant is not wandering far afield and is providing the interviewer with meaningful and useful material, do not interrupt him. He may reveal some important and relevant facets of his attitudes, behavior, and value system.

Reliance on Intuition

Some interviewers base their conclusions about an applicant on an intuitive feel, insufficiently supported by objective facts or evidence. These conclusions are rationalized by the argument that whenever the interviewer failed to follow his intuition, he usually regretted it. Research has strongly discredited this practice; it is completely unsystematic and invalid. The belief that intuition usually serves the individual correctly is totally fallacious. Our memory conveniently blocks out the many times it has failed us. Only insight and a complete understanding of what an applicant has done in the past will enable us to predict with some accuracy what he or she will do in the future.

Overemphasis on Initial Impression

It is only natural for us to form some initial impression when we meet an applicant. However, we must bear in mind that first impressions are not necessarily true indications of typical behavior response. As I have noted, some job applicants are nervous and ill at ease during the first few moments of the interview. Once rapport is established, however, the nervousness, discomfort, and awkwardness are soon dispelled.

Unfortunately, some interviewers unconsciously "lock in" their first impression of the job seeker. During the ensuing discussion, they look for information that will support and confirm their initial impression, and disregard any facts that contradict their premature assessment. To some extent, they fall victim to what might be referred to as "personnel tunnel vision." They are saying, in effect, "Don't confuse me with the facts; I have already made up my mind." Obviously, the only way to arrive at an objective hiring decision is to conduct a comprehensive Structured Selection Interview.

Injection of Stress Factors

Some people deliberately inject stress into the interview situation. They resort to techniques intended to upset or faze the candidate. They may subject the job applicant to verbal abuse; they may engage in sarcasm or facetiousness; or they may belittle, insult, or degrade the applicant and his qualifications and past accomplishments. On a less hostile but subtler level, they may ask trick questions whose purpose is to trap the applicant and to catch him off his guard.

Some campus recruiters interviewing potential sales trainees are fond of throwing a pencil at the candidate with the demand, "Sell me this pencil!" The underlying rationale behind this strategy, according to those who practice its counterproductive techniques, is the assumption that the job seeker is fundamentally untruthful, or at least evasive, and that only the stress interview will show the candidate as he really is.

Needless to say, the stress interview is a disastrous technique to follow. It almost assuredly destroys any rapport that may have been established, and it is exceedingly damaging to a company's public relations and its image as a desirable employer. Perhaps even more important, there is no shred of evidence that this technique generates accurate or objective information regarding the applicant. Indeed, a basic tenet of the Structured Selection Interview is the firm belief that only when the applicant is relaxed, comfortable, and made to feel at ease will a true picture of his behavior pattern emerge.

HOW TO CONDUCT THE STRUCTURED SELECTION INTERVIEW

Having reviewed some of the more frequent interviewing errors, many of which are committed on an unconscious level and therefore likely to be repeated, we are now ready to take an intensive look at how to interview properly; that is, how to conduct the Structured Selection Interview. However, before we can actually begin the interview, we must prepare for it.

Preparing for the Interview

The personnel professional should take preparatory steps before the interview.

1. *Review the job description.* The interviewer should have a very clear idea of what the job he is trying to fill is all about. It is therefore recommended that just before the interview begins he take another quick look at the written job description. During the interview, the applicant will no doubt have a number of questions about the job as well as about the company, and only a fully knowledgeable interviewer will be able to respond appropriately.

2. *Review the job specifications.* At the same time, the interviewer should review the job spcifications carefully. He should have a definite picture in his mind of all the essential qualifications the candidate should have for that particular job. It is often conceptually helpful to visualize the "ideal" candidate. When it is time to make a final decision, the interviewer can compare the actual applicant with

the perfect candidate he has imagined to determine the closeness of the fit.

3. *Review the application and the reference checks.* In preparing for the interview, it is most important that both the application form and the information obtained from the telephone reference checks be reviewed thoroughly. Items on the application may require further elaboration, time gaps in the applicant's work history may need to be explained, and the reasons the job candidate left previous positions may require clarification.

Furthermore, the interviewer may have been alerted to potential problems as a result of his telephone reference checks. For example, he may have been told that the applicant was fired because he was careless on the job, made frequent errors, and required too much supervision. Forewarned, the personnel specialist will wish to probe this particular aspect of the candidate's qualifications very carefully during the interview.

4. *Determine areas of inquiry.* As a result of having reviewed the application form and the telephone reference checks, chances are the interviewer will want to explore particular areas in the candidate's background in greater depth. Specific items on the application or so-called "caution flags" may raise questions in the interviewer's mind that should be clarified to his complete satisfaction.

The interviewer may wonder why the candidate spent five years attending college for a four-year undergraduate degree; why he stated on the application that there was no advancement to be had with his present company; why he progressed so modestly in salary, despite the fact that he worked for his company for five years; and what he means when he states on the application that he wishes to leave his present organization because of "policy differences."

I suggest that you circle any areas requiring elaboration on the application form or that you make a note to remind you to explore the area in question.

5. *Provide for appropriate surroundings.* If rapport is to

be established and the applicant put at ease, proper attention must be given to the surroundings in which the interview is to take place. The setting need not be luxurious. However, an attractive, comfortable, and well-lighted private office is conducive to an in-depth discussion.

Care should also be taken to prevent people from interrupting the interview and, if at all possible, telephone calls should be held off. Interruptions are counterproductive. They break the personnel specialist's train of thought and may cause him to miss some meaningful information. Also, some applicants take advantage of interruptions in the interview to restructure and change their story, particularly if they realize that the interviewer is getting uncomfortably close to uncovering something unfavorable to their candidacy.

6. *Allocate enough time.* Sometimes the interview is too short and superficial, perhaps because inadequate time was set aside for it. The personnel specialist may be under a good deal of pressure to keep the discussion brief, with the result that only very general and surface information is obtained. He should not space his appointments too closely. Instead, he should see to it that enough time is allotted for each interview.

THE SIX STEPS IN THE STRUCTURED SELECTION INTERVIEW

Thoroughly prepared, we are ready to launch the Structured Selection Interview. There are six distinct steps that constitute the Structured Selection Interview that the personnel practitioner should follow in sequence. The six steps are listed and then explored in detail. They are:

1. Personal introduction and welcoming the applicant to the company's offices.
2. Engaging in some small talk.
3. Obtaining relevant interview information.

4. Providing the applicant with information about the company and the job.
5. Responding to the applicant's questions.
6. Concluding the interview.

Step #1. Introduction and Welcome

The Structured Selection Interview should begin with the personnel professional introducing himself or herself to the applicant and extending a warm and sincere welcome. The first few moments of the interview are always very important. They get the discussion off the ground and set the stage. Therefore the interviewer should recognize the necessity of establishing good rapport with the applicant right from the beginning. As I have pointed out, only if the applicant is relaxed, comfortable and at ease will he be able to present himself in a true light.

The interviewer can contribute significantly toward establishing the right type of rapport by his own manner and demeanor. He should be sincerely interested in the applicant and eager to hear what he or she has to say. He should be cordial and friendly while remaining businesslike. And he should let the candidate know by his manner that he does not intend to be critical, moralistic, or judgmental.

Step #2. Small Talk

As a means toward establishing the right type of rapport, I suggest a few minutes of small talk on a casual, neutral subject. The topic is immaterial. The purpose of the small talk is to loosen up and relax the applicant.

The skilled interviewer will choose a subject less trite than the weather. A relatively innocuous biographical item can be selected from the application form to get the interview off the ground. For example, the interviewer may note that both the applicant and he attended the same high school. A few moments spent in reminiscence should establish the desired rapport. Many interviewers have a particular "ice breaker" question, such as, "Did you have any difficulty finding our office?" In any case, steps #1 and #2—Introduction and Welcome and Small Talk—should take no more than three or four minutes.

Step #3. Obtaining Relevant Information

Now that we have established the right conversational relationship, we are ready to move into the most essential part of the interview—obtaining relevant and job-related information. On what key areas will we wish to focus? Three categories need to be explored thoroughly: work experience, educational background, and personal factors directly related to the position. These three categories can be further broken down as follows:

WORK EXPERIENCE

1. What were the applicant's specific duties and responsibilities in each of his (her) previous jobs?
2. How successful was the applicant in each job and what were his (her) precise accomplishments?
3. What progress did he (she) make in his (her) jobs and what failures did he (she) encounter?
4. What did he (she) like and dislike in each of his (her) previous positions?
5. What caused the applicant to leave each of his (her) former jobs?

EDUCATIONAL BACKGROUND

1. How successful was the applicant academically?
2. What were his (her) best and worst subjects?
3. In which campus activities did he (she) engage and why?
4. How did he (she) finance his (her) education?
5. What was his (her) attitude toward education?

PERSONAL FACTORS

1. How does the applicant perceive himself (herself)?
2. What does he (she) regard to be his (her) outstanding strengths and limitations?
3. What are the applicant's long-range career goals and objectives?
4. How does the applicant plan to further his (her) own self-development?

Answers to these important questions can best be obtained by selecting items from our list of Tested Questions for the Structured Selection Interview, which may be found in Appendix A. Looking at the list, you can see that there are far more questions than there would be time to ask them. Therefore, select whatever questions from each of the three categories that you would find particularly useful and with which you would feel comfortable, and start to use them during your very next interview. Initially, you may want to put some of them on a small index card and unobtrusively refer to them during the course of the interview. In all probability, however, before too long this practice will no longer be necessary; asking these questions will become second nature.

To obtain the most relevant information possible in the shortest time possible, start this critical part of the interview by exploring the applicant's past employment history in *inverse* chronological order, beginning with his *present job first.* If the candidate is not employed, begin with his most recent job and work backward.

There are several important reasons for following this strategy. To begin with, the applicant's work history probably represents the most relevant single aspect of his qualifications, and he undoubtedly expects to be questioned in depth about it. Consequently, by focusing early in the interview on his actual work experience, you will probably augment the rapport you established during steps #1 and #2.

Discuss the applicant's present position (or last one if he is not employed) first because it is probably the most relevant. Most people work themselves up from positions of lesser scope and responsibility to assignments at an ever higher level. The candidate's present job—or certainly a recent one—is usually the best and most important he has held. It is therefore not a good use of one's time, particularly when considering an experienced applicant, to focus initially on his very first or earlier positions. As we shall see in a later chapter, if the candidate's recent work experience has been unsatisfactory, you will probably wish to terminate the interview earlier than originally anticipated and save yourself some time.

Ask the candidate all the questions you have to until you understand precisely how the applicant functioned in his present or last job and all the related information has been clarified to your complete satisfaction. Only then should you move on to the preceding job. Once again, you will wish to obtain a complete understanding of the candidate's total performance in that position before proceeding to the job before that. It is not advisable to jump in the interview from a discussion of one job to another. To do so would destroy the smooth sequential continuity of the interview and prevent the personnel practitioner from getting a very clear picture of just how the applicant performed in each of his various assignments.

Once all the applicant's former positions have been fully explored, lead the discussion to a review of his or her educational background. This is another area the applicant fully expects to discuss. Select several inquiries from the list of Tested Questions, and after you are satisfied on this point, move into the area of personal factors.

By now, the interview should be proceeding quite smoothly, conversation should be flowing freely, and—provided you have been able to convey to the applicant the feeling that you fully accept him and are interested in what he is saying—there should be a high degree of rapport. This condition will help to facilitate a discussion of the subtler, more sophisticated, information that is usually generated by the items listed in the personal factors category of the list of Tested Questions for the Structured Selection Interview.

Here is where you will be able to obtain more in-depth and comprehensive information about the applicant in such vital areas as what he believes to be his outstanding strengths, his developmental needs, and his career and personal goals and objectives. A thorough knowledge and understanding of these personal factors are often of critical importance in effective personnel selection and placement. They enable the qualified applicant to be assigned to a position in which he or she will be able to make a worthwhile contribution to the company and at the same time realize a high degree of personal job satisfaction.

Last, after asking everything you want to, give the applicant the opportunity to offer any information he regards as relevant that may not have been covered. One good way to invite such a response might be to say, "Well, Mr. Stevens, I believe I have asked you everything I think I need to know. Is there anything else regarding your background that we have not covered and that you feel would be relevant?" Quite often, the applicant will take advantage of this invitation to offer some additional information that might have an important bearing on his eligibility.

GETTING THE APPLICANT TO TALK

Every interviewer has come across the applicant who is exceedingly hard to draw out in conversation. Despite the fact that rapport seems to have been quite well established and a relaxed, cordial, and nonpressured interview atmosphere prevails, the applicant is exceedingly contained and relatively noncommunicative, responding to questions with short, cryptic answers. This can be frustrating, particularly if on the basis of the application form the interviewer believes the candidate to possess promising qualifications. If all his attempts to get the applicant to "open up" fail, what should he do? I suggest that he use the following techniques to draw out the applicant more fully and to get him to elaborate on his qualifications.

The Generalized Approach

A good way to initiate discussion of a new topic—for example, a particular job—is to use the generalized or nonspecific approach. Let us assume the interviewer has established rapport and now wishes to explore the candidate's present employment. He might launch the discussion by using a nonspecific statement such as: "I see that you are working for Associated Food Distributors. I wonder if you could tell me something about your job there?" Another illustration of this technique would be to say: "Now, Mr. Stevens, your last job was with the Universal Rubber Company. Let's talk about that."

The generalized approach is intentionally broad and ambiguous. It permits the applicant to select the significant aspects of the topic under discussion and to elaborate on those aspects. In so doing, he frequently reveals his underlying attitudes and value system. He may start his discussion by saying: "Well, I have an interesting job and I like the company very much, but it's an awfully static organization and there really is not much of an opportunity to move ahead." Having said this, he has told the interviewer that one of his key needs is the chance for job advancement. Subsequent interview information should confirm this need. A completely different interpretation would be drawn from the statement: "It's a good job as jobs go, but the pay is kind of low."

Open-Ended Questions

The interviewer should never use a question that can be answered by a yes or no. Asking whether the applicant likes his present job will probably yield a yes or no response, which doesn't tell the personnel specialist much. We need to know what aspects of the job appeal to the candidate and what aspects he dislikes. Questions that begin with who, what, where, when, why, and how—the five *w*s and the *h*, as they are referred to in many writing and journalism courses—are much more likely to draw out the applicant and result in useful information. Note that many of the Tested Questions for the Structured Selection Interview in Appendix A are open ended; for example, "What were some of your chief accomplishments while you were with the Apex Engineering Corporation?"

The Interview Pause

The experienced personnel professional has learned that a very effective way to generate additional interview data is by the deliberate and judicious use of silence—an intentional pause—during the course of the interview. The following scenario will demonstrate this useful technique. The interviewer has just asked the applicant why he wishes to leave his present company and the candidate has said that he sees little chance of moving ahead in the organization. At this point, the interviewer should remain silent for a few moments, thus clearly signaling to the applicant that he wants more information. The applicant will ordinarily pick up the cue and expand his answer. In this instance, he might say that his superior is only a few years older than he and that the growth rate of the company is such that advancement opportunities are apt to be quite limited in the near future.

Self-Evaluation Questions

Meaningful information is likely to be generated when the interviewer uses the self-evaluation type of question. In this technique, the candidate provides the interviewer with additional insight into how the applicant views himself and his past achievements. He is thus furnishing data on such important factors as motivational needs, attitudes, values, and personal maturity. As the list of Tested Questions will indicate, typical questions would be: "What do you believe to be your chief contribution during your three years with Associated Textiles?" "How do you think college contributed to your career development?" "What major trends do you see emerging in your field of work?" and "How do you evaluate your strengths and your developmental and growth needs?"

Applicant Acceptance

One of the best ways to generate valuable interview information is to demonstrate psychological acceptance of the applicant. As has already been pointed out, the interviewer should never be critical, moralistic, or judgmental, or in any way reflect disapproval of the applicant or of any of his actions. So long as the applicant feels that the interviewer is interested in him as a person and in what he has to say, he will be inclined to clarify all aspects of his qualifications fully. After all, the applicant is talking about his favorite subject—himself. There are several effective ways to signal an interest in the applicant. Among them are nodding one's head, showing a faint smile, and uttering such phrases as "that's interesting," "I see," and "tell me more." Even an occasional "Umm" or "Oh!" will encourage the applicant to elaborate.

The Reflective Technique

Perhaps the most successful technique of all is the reflective technique. Here, the interviewer will reflect, or restate, the feeling and emotional aspects—but not the content—of what the applicant has just expressed. The following illustration will demonstrate this valuable technique.

> *Interviewer:* What do you particularly like about your present job?

Applicant:	Oh, I like the fact that I am pretty much on my own.
Interviewer:	You operate rather independently and without too much close supervision.
Applicant:	Yes, that's right. So long as you meet established goals and targets, they don't care too much about how you organize your work. And I really enjoy the fact that I can plan and arrange my day as I think it should be done. As a matter of fact, I've come across a number of better ways to get the job done just by trying different techniques.

Note that the interviewer is rephrasing and rewording the applicant's statements to reflect their *emotional* and *feeling* aspects. In using this technique, however, it is important *not* to use the applicant's identical phraseology. Most personnel professionals report that it takes a certain amount of practice to perfect this technique, but that once it has been mastered it is highly effective.

ADDITIONAL INTERVIEW AIDS

A number of additional aids can be suggested to help you obtain enough information about the applicant to make an objective decision. These will be listed below.

1. *Keep control over the interview.* The interviewer should always direct the interview, steering it in the proper direction without dominating it autocratically. He must be sure to ask all the questions he feels are necessary. If the applicant attempts to redirect the discussion—perhaps because the interviewer is asking astute and penetrating questions that the candidate fears will result in an adverse decision—the interviewer should tactfully but firmly bring the discussion back on target.

2. *Record key information as it is supplied.* Take notes during the interview, preferably on a separate sheet of paper. Trusting to one's memory is a poor practice; a great deal of meaningful information can be lost in the process. Appropriate notes that can be reviewed in detail by the interviewer will make the applicant's qualifications more apparent and permit their more accurate evaluation. In addition, applicants are usually favorably impressed by an interviewer taking notes, interpreting this act as a sign of definite interest on the part of the company. It may encourage them to elaborate on their credentials.

3. *Personalize the tested questions.* Personalize the Tested Questions you choose to draw out the applicant, using a language style and level that is both comfortable and natural to you and appropriate to the interview situation.

4. *Always get exact dates of employment.* It is imperative to get the applicant's precise dates of employment, including months and years. The years alone cannot give you a full account of all the applicant's time since he left school. Where accurate chronological records were not obtained, some highly negative information was often obscured, such as the fact that the applicant held other positions he preferred not to disclose because his references would be detrimental.

5. *Check inconsistencies carefully.* If the interviewer is not satisfied with the applicant's answer to a particular question, or if he wishes additional clarification, he should never drop the matter. He must pursue the point and clarify the issue until he is completely satisfied. Failure to follow through on a critical point may result in not obtaining information that could have a vital bearing on the final selection decision.

6. *Take enough time to conduct a thorough interview.* Some interviewers periodically feel themselves under time pressure. They rush through the interview, obtaining only cursory information. Since unqualified applicants were screened out in Steps 3 and 4 (Chapters Five and Six), the

remaining applicants presumably represent promising candidates who should be interviewed thoroughly. Regrettably, all too often hiring decisions are made on the basis of
incomplete information.

7. *Talk less, listen more.* Throughout Step 3 of the
Structured Selection Interview, the interviewer's job is to
gather information dealing with the applicant's qualifications. To do this he must learn to be a good listener. As we
saw earlier in this chapter, one of the cardinal errors in
employment interviewing is the tendency on the part of
some interviewers to talk too much and not listen enough.
Therefore, our motto here is "talk less, listen more."

8. *Avoid leading questions or giving preferred interview answers.* Many interviewers inadvertently give away
the answers they are looking for or are prepared to accept.
Instead of asking open-ended questions, they feed the applicant the answers they expect. Some illustrations will
clarify this point.

> Tell me about your leadership activities on campus.
> *The applicant may not even have had any leader-
> ship activities, but will quickly make some up.*

> I see you majored in Marketing. I guess that is be-
> cause you have always been interested in sales. *He
> may have selected the major only because it was
> regarded on campus as an "easy" one; the inter-
> viewer has just helped the applicant to make a
> career decision.*

> Do you want to leave your present job because you
> are dissatisfied with the salary, or because you see
> little chance for advancement? *Neither of these two
> reasons may be the precipitating one; the reason
> could be entirely different.*

> A better way to phrase these questions would be:
> "Tell me about some of your campus activities."
> "Why did you decide to major in Marketing in college?"
> "Why do you want to leave your present job?"

Step #4. Discussing the Company and the Position

Once the interviewer has obtained all the necessary information regarding the applicant, it is time to give the applicant comparable and full facts about the company and the position. The personnel professional must always bear in mind that staffing is fundamentally a two-way street. The company must be convinced that the applicant is truly qualified for the position that is open, and the applicant must feel that the company and the position meet his or her career goals and needs. Unless there is an appropriate fit, neither party will be satisfied.

The interviewer must therefore be as candid and as informative with the applicant as he expects the applicant to be with him. The candidate is certainly entitled to all pertinent information regarding the organization and the job. The position should be factually and accurately explained. Unfortunately, some interviewers dwell only on the positive aspects of the job, without ever mentioning some of the less desirable features. This is a serious error and may readily contribute to personnel turnover.

If the position entails periodic overtime, night, or weekend work, or if a degree of travel is required, such essential facts should be given to the applicant during the interview. If the candidate only learns about them after he starts the job, he may resign after a short period of time.

At this point in the Structured Selection Interview, salary is usually discussed. Some positions pay a fixed salary or wage and allow no deviation from that rate. Increasingly, however, many jobs have a stipulated salary range, subject to the specific evaluation of the qualifications of the particular applicant. As a result, the interviewer may find himself engaged in salary negotiations with the applicant. At that time he should ask himself, "What is this individual worth to our company if I take into account all his qualifications and our organization's internal salary structure?"

In many instances it is advisable to show the job to the applicant before making a selection decision. In personnel staffing, one picture is frequently worth a thousand words. Sometimes applicants find it difficult to envision themselves in a given job setting. A lot of companies have found it helpful to allow a sales trainee applicant to spend a day out in the field with an experienced sales representative so that he may have a clearer picture of what his life would be like as a sales representative for the organization.

Of critical importance at this point is that the interviewer be fully convinced that the applicant is really interested in the company and the position and that he is strongly motivated to join the organization. If that is not the case, the applicant should not be considered for employment. Some companies have learned to their distress that many people are willing to try a job. If it fails to meet their requirements, they resign and add to the organization's personnel turnover. Therefore, the interviewer should be convinced and assured by the applicant, who can articulate his reasons, that he really wants the position. If the interviewer is not convinced, he can extend an invitation to the applicant to think it over and return at a later date if he wants to.

Step #5. Responding to the Applicant's Questions

The applicant probably has a number of questions he or she would like answered. Often a degree of give and take ensues between the interviewer and the applicant in which additional areas are clarified by both parties. Such topics as the company's policy on salary increases, the possible existence of tuition refund programs, and key employee benefits are discussed at this stage.

Step #6. Ending the Interview

When the interviewer feels that all his questions have been answered satisfactorily and the candidate has had his questions answered, it is time to bring the interview to an end. This is best done by the interviewer, who should express his appreciation to the applicant for the time he has given the company. Also, the interviewer should inform the applicant of the procedure by which the company will arrive at its selection decision.

For most lower level positions, especially where many applicants have been interviewed, it is perfectly proper and appropriate to tell the applicant that the company will evaluate his qualifications carefully and compare them with those of other candidates. If his credentials come closest to the company's requirements, he will be notified accordingly. It is a sound practice to give the applicant some outside date—say, four to five days—and to tell him that if he has not heard from the company by that time, he should assume that another applicant has been selected.

A candidate who has applied for a more responsible, higher level position should be told that he will be notified of the organization's decision one way or another—again, within a specified period of time. In the interest of good public relations, some companies, particularly those in the consumer products area, have a standard policy of notifying all applicants by mail, regardless of the level of the position involved.

One strategic point should be stressed. If the personnel specialist is certain that the applicant is not qualified, the interview should be abbreviated. Let us assume, for example, that some fourteen minutes into the interview, during step #3—Obtaining Relevant Interview Information—we decide that the applicant is clearly not qualified for the job. There is no need to prolong the discussion, even though we originally allocated one full hour to the interview. Such situations are common. When they occur, the personnel specialist should "telescope" the interview by covering steps 4, 5, and 6 briefly and bringing the interview to a swift and convenient end.

nine

Step 6—Evaluating the applicant and reaching a decision

BY NOW WE HAVE a great deal of valuable information. If properly evaluated, it should help the interviewer immeasurably to arrive at an objective and accurate final selection decision. Now that the candidate has left the interviewer's office, he is ready to thoroughly analyze all the facts that have been gathered. The telephone checks and the Structured Selection Interview must now be objectively rated.

As suggested in the preceding chapter, in arriving at a decision, it is advisable to have a concept of the "ideal" or "perfect" applicant. After the real candidate has left, his credentials can be compared with those of the "ideal" applicant to see how good a fit there is between them. To help make the comparison, it is a good idea to consult the job description and the job specifications again in order to be completely familiar with them.

To arrive at an objective and accurate final evaluation, I suggest you use the Interviewer Rating Form (Figure 8). Note that the general qualifications discussed in the chapter on Psychological Insights in Selecting Personnel— namely, basic abilities, personal characteristics, and character traits—are all listed for the interviewer's evaluation.

Not all qualifications that appear on the Interviewer Rating Form will be applicable for all candidates. Therefore, rate only those that are both job related and necessary, in accordance with equal employment opportunity requirements. Needless to say, to rate a typist, we would not ordinarily need to consider organizational skills, interpersonal assertiveness, or leadership, qualifications that would be essential for a potential manager.

To recapitulate, the interviewer should carefully evaluate all the information he has obtained on the applicant, completing the Interviewer Rating Form and being sure to provide supportive data for his conclusions in the column marked Comments. Particular attention should be given to input on the applicant's strong and weak points as they pertain to the position for which he is being considered. Finally, the interviewer will need to arrive at an overall numerical rating. For the sake of convenience, I prefer a five-point rating scale such as this:

OVERALL RATING

1	Outstanding	Applicant possesses all the necessary qualifications and has virtually no undesirable characteristics.
2	Very Good	Applicant is well qualified, but not outstanding. He or she may

Figure 8. Interviewer rating form.

Applicant's Name _____ Date _____ 19 ____

Position _____ Department _____

QUALIFICATIONS

(Check and rate only those that apply to position in question)

BASIC ABILITIES

	Superior	Very Good	Good	Fair	Poor	Comments
☐ Intelligence & Mental Alertness						
☐ Job Knowledge & Skills						
☐ Education						
☐ Experience						
☐ Organizational Skills						
☐ Communication Skills						
☐ Energy Level						

PERSONAL CHARACTERISTICS

☐ Inter-Personal Skills (poise & bearing)						
☐ Manner & Attitude						
☐ Inter-Personal Assertiveness						
☐ Initiative, Drive & Resourcefulness						
☐ Maturity						
☐ Motivation & Ambition						

CHARACTER TRAITS

- ☐ Stability
- ☐ Industry
- ☐ Perseverance
- ☐ Ability to Get Along With Others
- ☐ Confidence & Self Reliance
- ☐ Leadership

List applicant's strong points for this position

_____

_____

List applicant's weak points for this position

_____

_____

OVERALL RATING

	1 Outstanding	2 Very Good	3 Average	4 Fair	5 Unsatisfactory
For This Position					
Potential for Advancement					

Recommendation to Employ ☐ Yes ☐ No

Rated By _____

be expected to perform quite well on the job, in spite of some minor deficiencies in basic abilities, personal characteristics, or character traits. Since these limitations are minor, however, they do not pose a problem.

3 Average   In most respects, this applicant is pretty average. Nevertheless, in the absence of a better candidate, he or she may be hired.

4 Fair   This is a marginal or borderline applicant about whom there is some serious doubt with regard to his or her ability to perform satisfactorily. As a result, this person should be rejected in favor of a better candidate.

5 Unqualified   This applicant is unsatisfactory. The candidate is seriously deficient in one or more of the critical qualifications for the position and must be rejected, regardless of the need to fill the job.

Besides using this scale, the interviewer should rate candidates for professional or managerial assignments on potential for growth and development, where it would appear applicable, since these people are frequently expected to advance within the company.

Now comes the ultimate decision: whether to recommend the candidate for employment or to reject him from further consideration.

THREE IMPORTANT CONSIDERATIONS

Rate accurately. The interviewer must evaluate the candidate realistically and objectively, offering evidence to substantiate his conclusions and decision. Some interviewers unconsciously rate a given applicant higher than his qualifications warrant because of pressure to fill the position. This practice is unwise. Applicants should be evaluated properly. The personnel professional should never accept a marginal candidate in the fervent hope that with time and training he can be brought to a satisfactory level of performance.

Avoid both underqualified and overqualified people. Most personnel people are aware of the danger in hiring a candidate who does not come up to standards. It is equally poor practice to hire an overqualified person. Such an individual may take the job as a temporary expedient to gain employment and get in out of the rain, but before too long he will leave to accept one more in keeping with his qualifications. Hiring underqualified or overqualified people invariably contributes to a company's personnel turnover.

Do not compromise on standards. What should the interviewer do when he or she is in a quandary and has some real doubts about whether or not to hire the applicant? This situation occurs fairly often. My own feeling is, if in doubt, reject him. Do not take a chance that once he is hired, he may turn out better than expected. Presumably the applicant wanted the job and therefore was at his best in presenting himself at the interview. If under these circumstances, he still caused the interviewer to have serious reservations, hiring him will probably be a grave mistake. Select another applicant or continue the recruiting process, rather than compromise or lower your standards.

It is helpful to look at employment statistics in clarifying this issue. Statistically, an applicant, once hired, turns out to be *less* satisfactory more often than he turns out to be better than expected. To reiterate, when there is reasonable doubt, reject the candidate.

SCREENING VERSUS ACTUAL SELECTION

As indicated in the Preface, this book is directed toward two types of readers: the personnel specialist responsible for providing *staff* support for his or her organization in the recruiting and employment area and the operating manager who may not have the services of an on-site personnel department available and must handle the entire employment function without such help.

Generally speaking, the full-time professional personnel specialist will follow the steps indicated in our Sequential Selection System, *screening out* the unqualified candidate and *recommending* one or several qualified individuals to the hiring manager or executive for a final decision. In practice, therefore, once the personnel specialist is satisfied that a promising applicant has been secured, he or she should refer the person to the hiring manager or executive, giving the specific reasons the candidate warrants serious consideration. In discussing the candidate's qualifications with the hiring manager, it is often helpful for the personnel specialist to indicate on the Interviewer Rating Form how the candidate's qualifications match the specifications for the position in question.

In some instances, the personnel specialist may be authorized to do the *final* hiring; often, for example, for relatively junior positions. As a rule, however, the hiring manager or executive makes the final decision. During the final selection interview the operating manager must verify the applicant's professed technical or professional knowledge and competence and confirm that he or she does have the claimed expertise.

Obviously, the accounting manager or data processing director can best judge the supposed technical competence of an accounting or programming job applicant. On the other hand, without a personnel department to recruit and screen, the entire burden of the employment process falls on the shoulders of the operating manager.

Final Selection Steps

Before a firm offer of employment is extended to an applicant, because of the nature of the work involved, it is often highly advisable that he undergo a medical examination by a physician retained by the company. For obvious reasons, the candidate should not see his personal physician, who is more interested in the patient than in the company. Also, the company must sometimes verify that the applicant has the proper license or certification for the position; for example, when employing a registered nurse, chauffeur, or licensed electrician.

Rejecting the Unqualified Applicant

As a matter of policy, I recommend most strongly that a job applicant rarely, if ever, be told the reason for his rejection. There are several sound reasons for this strategy. To begin with, it would frequently be awkward, if not tactically impossible, to give the applicant the real reason for his rejection. Some applicants are hostile or aggressive; others have antisocial tendencies or highly negative behavior traits; still others have unsatisfactory employment records they are prepared to defend to the hilt. Many applicants are well prepared with excuses and rationalizations to explain these unsatisfactory records.

For an interviewer to explain why the applicant was rejected would be a fruitless strategic error. Frustration at being rejected might be expressed by anger and aggressive behavior or, at the very least, a time-consuming argument is likely to take place, which the interviewer cannot win. Therefore, *never* reject the applicant. Instead, convey the impression that the applicant was not found wanting or unqualified. Rather, someone else simply approximated the desired qualifications more closely.

ten

The case
of Harry Nelson,
office supervisor

IN THIS FINAL chapter, we shall put into practice some of
the concepts of the Sequential Selection System. In a simu-
lation especially developed for the book, you will be in-
vited to consider the qualifications of Harry Nelson, who is
applying for the position of office supervisor for a fictitious
organization, which we shall call the Universal Life Insurance Company of New York City.

Mr. Nelson, whose application form appears in Figure 9,
was referred by an employment agency with which you
listed the opening and with which you have dealt successfully for several years. A job description and a job specification for the position of office supervisor appear on the opposite page. After reviewing Mr. Nelson's application, the job
description, and the job specification, study and evaluate

JOB DESCRIPTION
Office Supervisor, Policy Records Department
Universal Life Insurance Company

Reporting to the office manager, supervises and coordinates the activities of approximately twelve to fourteen clerical employees who prepare, check, and assemble life, health, and accident insurance policy records. Opens, reviews, and distributes incoming mail; determines proper work procedures; assigns duties to employees and frequently examines their work for accuracy, neatness, and timeliness; and maintains efficient flow of work by evaluating and, where necessary, revising the department's procedures and adjusting errors. Trains new employees and updates and develops their clerical skills. Exercises some degree of independent judgment in making decisions affecting employees and the work of the Policy Records Department, although predominant responsibility for this function rests with the office manager. Recommends the employment of new personnel as well as possible promotions, transfers, or discharges and offers suggestions regarding salary increases for personnel. May prepare special reports for management's consideration. Provides leadership necessary to motivate clerical employees and creates and maintains harmony and high morale among personnel.

JOB SPECIFICATION
Office Supervisor, Policy Records Department
Universal Life Insurance Company

Successful candidate for this position must be a college graduate, preferably with a degree in Business Administration or Accounting and a minimum of approximately three to five years of supervisory experience performing a related office administrative function over clerical personnel. Must demonstrate a high degree of self-confidence and have the personal qualifications needed to direct and supervise the activities of clerical employees effectively.

Figure 9. Application for employment for Harry C. Nelson, front. The reverse side of the application is on the opposite page.

APPLICATION FOR EMPLOYMENT

DATE ___October 19, 1975___

NAME (print)___Harry C. Nelson___   TELEPHONE Home:___649-8932___
                                                            Office:___742-6900-___
                                                                              ×49

ADDRESS ___712 Avenue "D"___   ___Brooklyn___   ___N.Y.___   ___11513___
              STREET   CITY   STATE   ZIP CODE

POSITION DESIRED___Office Supervisor___   SALARY EXPECTED $___15,C00___

                                          U.S. CITIZEN   PHYSICAL LIMITATIONS
DATE OF BIRTH___February 7___ 19_40_   ☒ YES   ☐ NO   ☐ YES   ☒ NO
(Federal Law Prohibits Discrimination Based on Age)

EDUCATION

Type of School	Name of School	Location of School	Major Subject	Graduate?	Last Year Attended
HIGH SCHOOL	Tilden High Schl.	Brooklyn, N.Y.	Academic Course	yes	1958
COLLEGE	University of Tampa	Tampa, Florida	Accounting	yes	1966
GRADUATE SCHOOL	St. John's University	Brooklyn, N.Y.	Management, Data Processing	no	1971

LIST ANY ADDITIONAL SKILLS, KNOWLEDGE, EXPERIENCE OR OTHER RELEVANT QUALIFICATIONS:

Vice President, New York Chapter of The Administrative

Management Society

(OVER)   ©Copyright 1975 by E.S. Stanton & Associates, Inc. New York, N.Y.

WORK EXPERIENCE
(Including U S Military Service, If Any) *

List names & addresses of all former employers beginning with the most recent.	Nature of Business	Dates of Employment				Position	Starting Salary	Final Salary	Reason for Leaving	Name of Superior
		From		To						
		Mo.	Yr.	Mo.	Yr.					
1 Associated Trucking New York City	trucking	9	71	Present		Assistant Office Manager	9,000	13,500	still there	Name: J. Houk Title Office Manager
2 Harris Dept. Store Allentown, Pa.	retail	7	70	9	71	Supervisor Accts. Receivable	6,500	8,000	advancement	Name H. Scott Title Comptroller
3 New Novelty Mfg.Co. Brooklyn, N.Y.	plastic novelties	2	68	3	70	Production Control Man	95	125	personality clash	Name T. Brown Title Production Mgr.
4 Universal Finance New York City	loan company	12	66	2	68	Collection Man	85	95	no future	Name R. Harry Title Manager
5 U.S. Air Force	military	8	58	7	62	A/1st	—	—	end of enlistment	Name Title

INDICATE BY NUMBER 1,3 WHICH EMPLOYERS YOU DO NOT WISH US TO CONTACT.

As part of our employment process, an investigation may be made with respect to an applicant's credit status, character, general reputation, personal characteristics and mode of living. Additional information as to the nature and scope of such a report, if made, will be provided upon the written request of the applicant.

Date October 19, 19 75 Signature *Harry C. Nelson*

* Do not ask in New Jersey

the verbatim transcripts of the two reference checks and complete the blank Telephone Reference Check forms given in Figures 10 and 11. Then review the transcript of the Structured Selection Interview that was conducted with Harry Nelson.

After these steps have been taken, complete the Interviewer Rating Form (Figure 12), evaluating the applicant's qualifications. Lastly, give your overall rating of the candidate and decide whether or not to recommend the employment of Harry Nelson. When you have finished, you can read how I have analyzed the strengths and limitations of our fictitious applicant, and determine for yourself how accurate you were in evaluating the applicant's qualifications and suitability for the position in question.

Transcript of Telephone Reference Check

Conducted with Mr. T. Brown, Production Manager, New Novelty Manufacturing Company, Brooklyn, New York, regarding Harry C. Nelson

Interviewer:	Mr. Brown?
Reference:	(Impatiently) Yes. Who is this?
Interviewer:	Mr. Brown, I'm Jack Henderson, personnel specialist with Universal Life Insurance Company and _____.
Reference:	(Impatiently) So, what is it you want of me?
Interviewer:	Well, Mr. Brown, I would like to verify some of the information given to us by Mr. Harry C. Nelson, who is applying for a position with our company.
Reference:	(Somewhat annoyed) Oh, if this is a reference check, I don't want to talk to you. These things are handled by our Personnel Department.
Interviewer:	Mr. Brown, I appreciate that, but frankly, you are the person I really want to talk to. I assume Mr. Nelson worked directly for you

	and I would greatly appreciate and value your opinion in this case.
Reference:	Well, OK, but make it fast, because I'm running a busy shop here.
Interviewer:	Thank you very much, Mr. Brown. Now, do you recall Mr. Nelson's dates of employment with you?
Reference:	(Somewhat disparagingly) Well, whatever they were, he was here too long! But I guess it must have been something like the early part of 1968 until the early part of 1970.
Interviewer:	I see. What was the nature of his job?
Reference:	Well, he was a production control man, or at least he tried to be. I don't know how much you know about production control functions, but his job was to expedite production and to get jobs through the shop on time; you know, straightening out bottlenecks, speeding up manufacturing, and kind of prodding and reminding foremen to get the work out on time.
Interviewer:	What did you think of Mr. Nelson's work?
Reference:	Well, he was not particularly good and I guess I never should have hired him, but when I first interviewed him he looked and sounded OK, and I thought he might work out. But I soon found out I was wrong.
Interviewer:	How was that, Mr. Brown?
Reference:	I guess the problem with Nelson was that he was just too nice a guy. He simply was not cut out for this kind of work. This is a fast-paced and highly pressured production environment, and it simply wasn't his cup of tea. You see, we are basically a production job shop, and we have to push as many as twenty-five to thirty different jobs out the door each and every day. And you have to be

able to put up with a lot of pressure and be real tough minded in this business to survive. I guess Nelson just didn't have it. As I said, maybe his problem was that he was too nice a guy. What kind of job did you say you had in mind for him, anyway?

Interviewer: As an office supervisor where he would be in charge of twelve or thirteen clerical employees.

Reference: (Disparagingly) Oh, you mean as a pencil pusher! Well I guess he might be able to do that, but as far as I was concerned he was not strong enough and forceful enough with the foremen and, at times, he let them walk all over him. Let me put it this way. He isn't a bad human being and I suppose I would love to have him as a next-door neighbor. But he wasn't forceful or assertive enough for this kind of business.

Interviewer: Mr. Brown, how would you describe his performance in comparison with other people?

Reference: Well, I tell you. It's hard to get real good production control men these days and, over the course of the years here, I've seen a lot of them come and go. Nelson was more or less like most of them—run of the mill.

Interviewer: What job progress did he make?

Reference: He didn't make any job progress at all! He had the same job when he left that he had when he came.

Interviewer: What were his earnings?

Reference: Oh, I don't know. That's some time back now, but I would say maybe $120 or $125 a week, in that neighborhood.

Interviewer: Why did Mr. Nelson leave your company?

Reference: (A bit annoyed) I fired him! I finally had it! He simply wasn't tough enough or firm enough and we were falling behind in our

	schedule. He wasn't able to push the foremen to get the work out fast enough.
Interviewer:	Would you reemploy Mr. Nelson?
Reference:	(Still annoyed) Well, if I fired him, I certainly wouldn't be inclined to bring him back again, would I, now?
Interviewer:	I guess not, Mr. Brown, but I wonder if you could tell me why not.
Reference:	Look, as I said, I really think you have to be somewhat of an SOB to do this job right and Nelson, as I told you, was too nice a guy and not strong enough for the job.
Interviewer:	Mr. Brown, what would you say are Mr. Nelson's strong points?
Reference:	Well, I don't know. I guess he's a very decent human being and all that. Let's see, well, he's reliable, dependable, and he certainly tries hard—you can say that for him.
Interviewer:	What about his limitations?
Reference:	Not tough enough! Not strong enough! He was much too easy with the foremen. Wasn't able to get them to move—not aggressive enough.
Interviewer:	How did he get along with other people?
Reference:	Well, as far as the foremen were concerned, he probably got along too well with them. As I said, you've got to be somewhat of an SOB to be a good production expediter.
Interviewer:	Could you comment on his attendance?
Reference:	That was all right.
Interviewer:	How about his dependability?
Reference:	He was a dependable sort of guy insofar as really trying. You have to give him credit for that.
Interviewer:	Was he able to take on responsibility?
Reference:	Well, I had to bail him out quite regularly. He wasn't too good at taking on the responsibilities I had in mind for him.

Interviewer:	Potential for advancement?
Reference:	I don't see where he could have gone with our company.
Interviewer:	How about the degree of supervision he needed?
Reference:	I was constantly riding him to get the job done.
Interviewer:	How about his overall attitude?
Reference:	Well, as I said, he certainly tried. I couldn't fault him on that. But trying simply isn't enough.
Interviewer:	Did Mr. Nelson have any personal difficulty that interfered with his work?
Reference:	You mean like gambling or drinking? No, nothing like that! He's a very solid citizen.
Interviewer:	Is there anything else of significance that we should know?
Reference:	Not that I can think of.
Interviewer:	Well, thank you very much, Mr. Brown. I really appreciate the time you were able to give me. Goodbye.

Transcript of Telephone Reference Check

Conducted with Mr. H. Scott, Comptroller, Harris Department Store, Allentown, Pennsylvania, regarding Harry C. Nelson

Interviewer:	Mr. Scott?
Reference:	Yes?
Interviewer:	Mr. Scott, this is Jack Henderson, personnel specialist with the Universal Life Insurance Company in New York City. I would like to verify some of the information given to us by Mr. Harry Nelson, who is applying for a position with our company.
Reference:	I'm afraid I can't give you any information by telephone. That's company policy. But if you will send me a letter, I will be pleased to respond promptly.

Interviewer:	Mr. Scott, I appreciate your company's policy, but I'm seeing a number of people for this particular position and will be arriving at a decision very soon. And with the delay that happens so often with the mails, it's just possible that Mr. Nelson might lose this opportunity.
Reference:	(Enthusiastically) Oh, did you say Nelson? Harry Nelson?
Interviewer:	Yes I did. Harry C. Nelson. He did work for you, did he not?
Reference:	Yes, indeed. He sure did. Well, normally I don't give out any telephone information, but if it's going to help Harry Nelson, I'd certainly like to do all I can. He was a superb man and I thought the world of him.
Interviewer:	I'm glad to hear that, Mr. Scott. Do you recall the dates of his employment with you?
Reference:	Well, let's see. It unfortunately wasn't very long. As far as I can recollect, he joined us during the summer of 1970 and left us in the fall, September I think it was, of the following year. Not a very long time, I'll grant you, but he did a superb job for us while he was here.
Interviewer:	What was the nature of his job with you?
Reference:	Well, Harry was the supervisor of our Accounts Receivable Department. That department sends out statements each month to our many charge account customers here in the store. And in that capacity he was responsible for supervising, well, I guess in those days it must have been about a dozen clerks, assigning them their work, checking it, and making sure that the statements went out on time.
Interviewer:	What did you think of his work?
Reference:	Oh, he did an outstanding job for us; in fact,

a lot better than most of the people I've had in that position, both before he came and after he left us. Let's see, he ran a very efficient department, introduced a couple of new procedures that improved things somewhat, and, as I recollect, even effected some cost savings for us insofar as he found that he could reduce the staff by one or two people and still get the work done.

Interviewer: How would you describe his performance in comparison with other people?

Reference: Well, as I just said, he was among the better men that I can recall, and I've been with the store for twenty-three years now.

Interviewer: What job progress did he make?

Reference: If you're talking about job advancement, he didn't make any because, after all, he was only with us for a shade over one year. But if you're talking about progress that he made in his work and in straightening out that department, that's a different story. When he first started with us, that department and its records were in pretty bad shape. But Harry sized up the problem pretty quickly. He worked very hard; he reorganized the operation—subject, of course, to my supervision and direction—and he straightened out the mess fairly soon.

Interviewer: I see. What were Mr. Nelson's earnings with you?

Reference: I don't recall exactly. It's several years back now, but I think it was probably in the $7,500 or $8,000 range.

Interviewer: Why did he leave your company, Mr. Scott?

Reference: Well, as you probably know, Harry is a New Yorker and while Allentown is not a small hick town by any means, it in no way compares with New York City. And I guess once a New Yorker, always a New Yorker. Also, as I think back, Harry's parents, or possibly his wife's parents, or maybe even both sets of parents lived in New York and I believe Harry was just interested in going back there. What apparently brought things to a head was that he got this offer to become an office manager, or assistant office manager—I don't recall exactly—back in New York at a salary that was somewhat higher than what he was earning here. And I suppose it all seemed to fit and Harry felt that he couldn't turn down the offer. We were very sorry to see him go.

Interviewer: Would you reemploy him, Mr. Scott?

Reference: We have a policy here at the store not to reemploy people who have left us.

Interviewer: I understand, but if you had no such policy, what would you do, Mr. Scott?

Reference: Oh, if we didn't have that policy, I'd be delighted to take him back. I'm not sure he would want to return to us. After all, the job is the same and I assume that he has made some good progress in his job and in his salary since he last worked for us. But yes, all things being equal, I'd love to take him back, if that's your question.

Interviewer: Mr. Scott, what would you say are Mr. Nelson's strong points?

Reference: Well, he certainly is a hard worker, very conscientious and thorough, and he was quite successful in gaining the respect of his people and in getting them to do good work for him.

Interviewer: What would you say are some of his limitations?

Reference: Limitations? That's hard to say. We didn't really find any limitations in him.

Interviewer: (Pause) No limitations at all?

Reference: Well, I'm not sure that he is executive material; that is, I don't know whether he could ever take over my job. After all, that requires a considerable background in accounting and Harry was not a CPA, as I am. But, of course, that was never a factor in the job he was in. In the particular job he was doing for us, he performed exceedingly well.

Interviewer: What do you mean when you say that he is not necessarily executive material?

Reference: That's hard to say. I mean Harry was certainly very good with the clerical people. I just don't know how effective he would be with high-level personnel—you know, buyers, merchandisers, and executives. But I mean we never had any problems with him as far as being able to handle the clerical help. I just don't know whether he's aggressive enough to go into higher management. But as I said, that in no way detracted from his ability to do a highly satisfactory job for us as an accounts receivable supervisor.

Interviewer: How did he get along with other people?

Reference: Oh, exceptionally well.

Interviewer: Could you comment on his attendance?

Reference: That was excellent.

Interviewer: How about his dependability?

Reference: Oh, that was outstanding. You could really rely upon him.

Interviewer: What about his ability to take on responsibility?

Reference: Within the limits of his job, everything that I gave him was always done right up to my expectations.

Interviewer: How about his potential for advancement?

Reference: Well, as I said, that situation did not come up in the year that he was with us.

Interviewer:	What about the degree of supervision he needed?
Reference:	I was always in overall charge, but within the framework of his unit, he was able to work pretty much on his own.
Interviewer:	What about Nelson's overall attitude?
Reference:	He had an excellent work attitude. As I said, he was conscientious, worked hard, and really had the store's interest at heart.
Interviewer:	Did he have any personal difficulties that interfered with his work?
Reference:	None whatsoever. This is a very solid individual.
Interviewer:	Is there anything else of significance that we should know?
Reference:	None that I can think of. I think you have a very good man in Harry Nelson and please give him my regards and best wishes.
Interviewer:	Well, thank you very much, Mr. Scott. I really appreciate the information you gave me. You have been most helpful. Goodbye.
Reference:	Goodbye.

Now that you have read the transcripts of the two telephone checks that were conducted, please complete the blank Telephone Reference Check forms that appear in Figures 10 and 11.

Then, carefully review the actual interview of our fictitious applicant, the transcript of which follows.

Figure 10. First telephone reference check for Harry C. Nelson.

HARRY C. NELSON
NAME OF APPLICANT

H. SCOTT   COMPTROLLER
PERSON CONTACTED   POSITION OR TITLE

HARRIS DEPARTMENT STORE   ALLENTOWN, PA.
COMPANY   CITY & STATE   TEL. NO.

1. I would like to verify some of the information given to us by
   (Mr., Miss, Mrs.) _____
   who is applying for a position with our company. What were
   the dates of his (her) employment with you?

   From _____ 19 ____ To _____ 19 ____

2. What was the nature of his (her) job?
   _____

3. What did you think of his (her) work?
   _____

4. How would you describe his (her) performance in comparison
   with other people?
   _____

5. What job progress did he (she) make?
   _____

6. What were his (her) earnings?
   _____

7. Why did he (she) leave your company?
   _____

8. Would you re-employ?
   ☐ Yes   ☐ No (Why not) _____

9. What are his (her) strong points?

_____

10. What are his (her) limitations?

_____

11. How did he (she) get along with other people?

_____

12. Could you comment on his (her)
    (a) attendance
    (b) dependability
    (c) ability to take on responsibility
    (d) potential for advancement
    (e) degree of supervision needed
    (f) overall attitude

_____

13. Did he (she) have any personal difficulties that interfered
    with his (her) work?

_____

14. Is there anything else of significance that we should know?

_____

_____ 19___   CHECKED BY _____
     DATE

167

Figure 11. Second telephone reference check for Harry C. Nelson.

HARRY C. NELSON
NAME OF APPLICANT   PRODUCTION MANAGER

T. BROWN
PERSON CONTACTED

NEW NOVELTY MANUFACTURING COMPANY   BROOKLYN, N.Y.
COMPANY   CITY & STATE   POSITION OR TITLE

TEL. NO.

1. I would like to verify some of the information given to us by (Mr., Miss, Mrs.) _____ who is applying for a position with our company. What were the dates of his (her) employment with you?

   From _____ 19____ To _____ 19____

2. What was the nature of his (her) job?

   _____

3. What did you think of his (her) work?

   _____

4. How would you describe his (her) performance in comparison with other people?

   _____

5. What job progress did he (she) make?

   _____

6. What were his (her) earnings?

   _____

7. Why did he (she) leave your company?

   _____

8. Would you re-employ?

   ☐ Yes   ☐ No (Why not) _____

168

9. What are his (her) strong points?

_____
_____
_____
_____

10. What are his (her) limitations?

_____
_____

11. How did he (she) get along with other people?

_____
_____

12. Could you comment on his (her)
    (a)   attendance
    (b)   dependability
    (c)   ability to take on responsibility
    (d)   potential for advancement
    (e)   degree of supervision needed
    (f)   overall attitude

_____
_____
_____
_____
_____
_____

13. Did he (she) have any personal difficulties that interfered
    with his (her) work?

_____
_____

14. Is there anything else of significance that we should know?

_____
_____
_____

_____   _____
DATE   19   CHECKED BY

169

Transcript of the Structured Selection Interview

Conducted by Jack Henderson, Personnel Specialist, Universal Life Insurance Company of New York City, with Harry C. Nelson, Applicant for the Position of Office Supervisor of the Policy Records Department

Interviewer: (Greeting the applicant) Mr. Nelson, I'm Jack Henderson. How are you? Welcome to Universal Life Insurance Company.

Applicant: Thank you, Mr. Henderson.

Interviewer: Won't you come right into my office and make yourself comfortable?

Applicant: Thank you very much, Mr. Henderson. (Glancing around him) Very attractive office you have here.

Interviewer: Thank you. I think it's most comfortable. Mr. Nelson, I've had a chance to look over your application and I noted that you attended school in Tampa, Florida. I have vacationed in the Miami area in the past, but have never gotten over to the west coast of Florida. How is it over there?

Applicant: Oh, it's very nice over there, too. Maybe not quite as busy or glamorous or flamboyant as the Miami Beach area. But the weather is about the same, and I believe there is more industry in Tampa than in Miami, which I guess is basically still a resort city. Tampa may not be a New York, but there is a fair amount of industry down there. Of course, I haven't seen it now for many a year. As a matter of fact, I haven't been down there since I graduated from college back in 1966. And I guess, like all places, it must have changed a great deal. But from what I read,

	they seem to have had a good deal of business growth in the last several years.
Interviewer:	Well, Mr. Nelson, Mrs. Powell of the employment agency spoke very highly of you, and I've had a good chance to study your application, which looks quite interesting.
Applicant:	Thank you, Mr. Henderson.
Interviewer:	I wonder if we could first talk a bit about your present company, Associated Trucking. Tell me something about the company and the job.
Applicant:	Well, Mr. Henderson, as you can see from my application, I have been with Associated Trucking now since September of 1971. I am an assistant office manager for what is essentially a medium-size interstate trucking company, and I'm responsible for about twelve to fourteen women who handle a variety of clerical tasks. The office is divided into several separate units, each one having a specific function. For example, I've got three women in the billing department, two in accounts receivable, and two handling the payroll. In addition, there is one woman whose job is a combination of purchasing and handling accounts payable, two in accounting, and two in customer service who handle adjustments and complaints.
Interviewer:	That's interesting, Mr. Nelson. Tell me, what is the extent of your responsibility and authority at Associated Trucking?
Applicant:	Well, of course, I report to Jack Houk. He's the office manager and the person in overall charge; I'm the number two man. But over the course of the years, Mr. Houk has dele-

gated a good deal of responsibility to me. For example, it's my job to assign the work to the people, to check it, and to make sure that everything is going the right way. Naturally, if there are any major problems I can't handle myself, Mr. Houk insists that he be kept fully informed and, of course, I consult with him. I have the usual personnel responsibilities insofar as I have a say in who gets hired and when someone has to be fired. I also recommend salary increases for my people to Mr. Houk.

Interviewer: I see, Mr. Nelson. Tell me, what are some of the things that you particularly like about your present job?

Applicant: Actually, I think I like just about everything in the job. I enjoy the active pace of the trucking business; I guess I kind of like running an efficient and well-managed operation; and I suppose I just generally like the field of office administration.

Interviewer: Good. Now perhaps we might turn the coin over. What are some of the things you dislike about the company and the job?

Applicant: Well, there really isn't very much I dislike about the job. I think the company has treated me well. As you can see from the application, my salary has advanced fairly, and Mr. Houk has given me the opportunity to put some of my own ideas into effect and to make certain improvements and changes in the office. And I've really enjoyed that.

Interviewer: Well, then, why do you want to leave?

Applicant: OK. I was about to come to that. Really the only thing I dislike about the job is the fact that there is not much of an opportunity to move ahead at Associated Trucking. As I see it. Mr. Houk, my superior, is only a few years older than I am. And, since he is the head man in the office, it is most unlikely that I will ever advance as long as he is there. And frankly, I don't see where Mr. Houk could go in the company. You see, Associated Trucking is a family-owned business and, quite candidly, I don't think Mr. Houk, who is not a member of the family, is going to go anywhere. It's not that I'm unhappy, or anything like that. It's just a matter of looking at my career over the long range and not seeing very much opportunity to move up with my present company.

Interviewer: I see. Well now, just prior to Associated Trucking, you were with the Harris Department Store in Allentown, Pennsylvania. Whatever took you down there, Mr. Nelson? I note that most of your life has been spent in New York.

Applicant: Yes, that's right. But when I left New Novelty Manufacturing Company in March of 1970, you may recall that we were in the midst of a recession. Frankly, jobs were scarce. Well, one day I saw an interestingly written ad in *The New York Times.* I answered it, one thing led to another, and I was hired.

Interviewer: And that was how you relocated to Allentown. Would you tell me something about your job with that organization?

Applicant: Yes, indeed. That was also a very fine job, and I really enjoyed the retailing field. I had never been with a department store before. Well, it was just a brand new experience for me. I was hired as accounts receivable supervisor at the store. Essentially, that meant being in charge of the credit department and seeing to it that the monthly bills were sent out on time to the store's charge account customers.

When I joined the organization, I found that the person who had the job before me had left rather abruptly, and the department was a mess. Many of the bills had not been sent out on time and the records had not been kept very accurately. Actually, the store recognized that there was a pretty major problem in that department. Well, I started in and the comptroller, a Mr. Scott, worked very closely with me for a while. He had to orient me to retailing in general and to the Harris Department Store in particular. As I said, I had had no experience whatsoever in the retailing area.

I can recall that I had to work some ungodly hours just to get things straightened out once again in that department. Finally, after a couple of weeks, we began to see the light at the end of the tunnel and were able to update our records and get all the bills sent out. After that, we launched a program whereby we started to communicate with those charge account customers who had been late in sending in their payments.

Interviewer: Sounds like you must have had a hectic time at the store. What did you especially like about your job at Harris?

Applicant: I guess I liked being thrown into a problem situation that required a little imagination and gave me the opportunity to improve on an ongoing system.

Interviewer: That sounds interesting, Mr. Nelson. Could you elaborate a bit on this?

Applicant: Yes, of course. When I first started, I could see that the store had an unnecessarily complex system of record keeping. In fact, it struck me as an archaic system. In each instance two different girls maintained what appeared to be a duplicate record system. I felt we could streamline the whole operation considerably and, by reorganizing the system, reduce the personnel by one or two people and still come up with a much more efficient way of doing things. As a matter of fact, I spent a good deal of time studying and analyzing the system, and then wrote a fairly elaborate report to my superior, the comptroller of the store, strongly recommending that we change the entire procedure.

Interviewer: What was his reaction to your suggestions?

Applicant: Well, at first he was dubious because the store, a fairly conservative organization, had done things pretty much the same way for quite a number of years. But the problems in the Accounts Receivable Department were so serious that I think Mr. Scott was willing to listen to practically any reasonably intelligent proposal that might improve the situation.

Interviewer: What were some of your specific responsibilities in the store?

Applicant: Yes. Essentially, my job was to distribute the work to the people. I guess there were about a dozen women, ranging in age anywhere from youngsters to fairly mature women. It was a basic office administrative function. My job was to assign the work to the people, check it, and make sure that the records were properly maintained and that the bills were sent out on time every month. Also, as in my present job at Associated Trucking, I'd have a hand in hiring new people and deal with any disciplinary problems that might come up—you know, things like excessive lateness and absenteeism. And I would work with Mr. Scott, the comptroller, and recommend salary increases for those of my people who I felt deserved them.

Interviewer: I see. How about some of the things that you did not particularly care for, Mr. Nelson?

Applicant: About the job or Allentown, Mr. Henderson?

Interviewer: Well, perhaps both.

Applicant: As far as the job went, I really enjoyed the busy pace in retailing. But I could see that it would be hard to get really good salary increases there, although actually I did not do badly at all, considering that I was only there a little over a year. You will note that I started at $6,500 and went up to $8,000, which they told me was quite unusual for a person who had not been with the store long.

You probably know, Mr. Henderson, that retailing does not pay a great deal of money, especially in the administrative area. The people who earn good money in a department store are the buyers and the merchandising specialists—certainly not the people on the administrative end. But if I may be somewhat immodest, my superior at Harris was very pleased with the way things improved in my department, and I know he went to bat for me with the store president to get me the raises I got.

Interviewer: How did your raises come?

Applicant: Actually quite rapidly for retailing. As I said, I started with $6,500 and, after six months, got a $1,000 raise, which they kept stressing was quite unusual. But as I said, Mr. Scott was quite pleased with the way the department had solved its problems, and I must say that he was very generous. That raise brought me to $7,500. Six months later I got another $500 raise, which then brought me to $8,000, my final salary there.

Interviewer: Did I infer you to say that you were not too happy with Allentown, Mr. Nelson?

Applicant: Well, yes, that's true. I mean there's nothing really wrong with Allentown. In fact, it's a rather pleasant community, and not that small. However, I guess I never really realized how much I liked New York until I left it. Not that I do that much—I mean theaters or concerts or anything like that—but I guess I just like the big city, that's all. Also, I have two elderly parents who live here. While I don't support them financially, they are getting on in years and are not in the best of health, and I was very pleased when an opportunity presented itself to return to New York.

Interviewer: Would you elaborate on that, please?

Applicant: Surely. Well, what happened was that an employment agency with whom I had registered shortly after I left the New Novelty Manufacturing Company called me one evening and told me about an opening with my present company. Although I had not really planned to leave Harris at that time, it was a chance to return to New York City, and the salary they offered was considerably higher than what I was earning in Allentown. The agency arranged a Saturday interview for me, and I drove over to talk to the people at Associated Trucking. After that, things moved quickly, because the following week they offered me the job. I gave notice to Harris, and we all went back to New York—back to the Big Apple.

Interviewer: (Looking at the application) Now, let us see, Mr. Nelson, I noted that there was a time gap between New Novelty Manufacturing Company and Harris Department Store. What did you do during those, let's see, I guess there was a period of some four months?

Applicant: Yes, I guess it was about three months or so.

Interviewer: What did you do during that time?

Applicant: Well, as I mentioned, there was sort of a mini recession going on, and I wanted to make sure that my next job would be the right one. I decided not to take just anything that happened to come along, but to hold out for a real career opportunity. Unfortunately, as things turned out, there weren't too many appropriate jobs available, and it did take somewhat longer than I had expected.

Interviewer: I see. Just before Harris, then, you worked for the New Novelty Manufacturing Company, the plastic novelties business, is it?

Applicant: Yes, that's right. This was a plastics manufacturing plant in Brooklyn that produced quite a variety of items—anything from plastic forks and knives to boxes and assorted things like shoehorns and toys—just about anything made of plastic that the company felt it could sell and make some money on.

Interviewer: What did you do there, Mr. Nelson?

Applicant: Well, my title was production control man, and my job was to expedite the various items through the plant. I was the liaison person between the Scheduling Department and the production foremen. To state it as best I can, I was supposed to push the jobs through the shop as quickly as possible.

Interviewer: What did you like about that assignment?

Applicant: Frankly, Mr. Henderson, not very much. I guess I really wasn't suited to a manufacturing environment. I soon realized that and, of course, ever since then I have been in office administration. Looking back now, I realize that I made a mistake in getting into the production control field. But I was rather young at that time and, like so many other young people just starting out, I thought it sounded interesting when I first heard about it.

Interviewer: You felt you weren't suited to a factory environment? What do you mean by that, Mr. Nelson?

Applicant: Well, I don't mean to sound unkind, but this was not a very successful or profitable company. In fact, New Novelty was quite marginal and had been losing money for a while. Also, to be perfectly candid, I don't think the company was well managed. They didn't seem to have any systems that really worked; there was a lot of chaos and confusion there; and promises were always being made to customers that couldn't be kept. My job was to try to expedite orders through the shop, but it was always a case of trying to fight a steep uphill battle.

Interviewer: Mr. Nelson, you indicated on the application that your reason for leaving New Novelty was a personality clash.

Applicant: Yes, that's true. The man I worked for, a Mr.

Brown, was the production manager. Again, I don't mean to sound unkind, but he was a very difficult person to work for. He was very nervous, and I can understand that, because he was under constant pressure. But he kind of expected miracles I don't think anyone could have performed to his satisfaction. There were simply too many problems in that plant and, no matter what anybody tried to do, I don't think anyone was ever really able to please Mr. Brown. You can see that I made a big mistake in accepting that job.

Interviewer: You regretted joining the company?

Applicant: Yes, I most certainly did. And, as you can see, I changed careers right after that, and think I have done quite well since that time in the field of office administration.

Interviewer: What, then, led up to your leaving New Novelty Manufacturing?

Applicant: Well, as I said, I saw that things were not coming along well and that this simply was not the right company or the right kind of work for me.

Interviewer: I see. Now before New Novelty, you had been with a loan company, Universal Finance, also here in New York City.

Applicant: Yes, that was my very first job right after graduating from the University of Tampa. They hired me as an outside collection man. This job consisted of chasing after delinquent accounts who had gotten consumer loans from the company and weren't paying them back.

Interviewer: You were not there very long, Mr. Nelson.

Applicant: Yes, that's true, Mr. Henderson. But that was my very first job out of school, and as you probably know, there's not much of a future in the consumer loan business. As a matter of fact, they had me in a very difficult and even dangerous neighborhood, and after one customer held a knife to my throat one day and warned me never to ring his doorbell again, I decided that I had better find myself a new job.

Interviewer: Yes, I guess that can be a rather harrowing experience. Well, let's talk a bit about your educational background, Mr. Nelson.

Applicant: Fine. Well, let's see. I graduated from high school here in New York and then volunteered for four years with the Air Force where I worked at various bases maintaining inventory on jet engine parts. For a while, I was stationed near Tampa, Florida. I liked the warm weather down there, so when I got out of the service I decided to take advantage of the GI Bill and enrolled at the University of Tampa, where I received a B.S. in accounting in 1966. And a couple of years later, I took two evening courses at St. John's University in their Graduate Division—one in management and one in electronic data processing.

Interviewer: What made you choose accounting, Mr. Nelson?

Applicant: Well, I liked accounting and I did rather well in my accounting courses, although I never intended to become an accountant as such. But I did feel that accounting would be most useful in any job in the area of business management and I wanted it as a kind of basic foundation.

Interviewer: Mr. Nelson, let me ask you a few more general questions. What do you consider to be

| | some of your more outstanding strengths and qualities? |

Applicant: Well, I'm not one to blow my own horn, but I guess when you're going for a job one has to, at least to some extent.

Interviewer: You're probably right, Mr. Nelson. (Pause)

Applicant: Let's see. Well, I guess I'm loyal, hardworking, and conscientious, and I suppose I'm good at organizing things, which essentially is what I've been doing for the last few years.

Interviewer: You have good administrative skills?

Applicant: Yes, I think so, Mr. Henderson. I guess I'm good at problem solving. When things go wrong in the office, I think I know how to analyze the problem, find out what went wrong, and come up with a good solution. I suppose that is what happened at Harris Department Store. And we have had similar situations at Associated Trucking, although certainly not as serious as the situation I found at Harris when I first went down to Allentown.

Interviewer: My next question may be somewhat harder, Mr. Nelson. Let's turn that coin over. You have told me about your strong points, now how about some of your limitations and areas in which you would like to improve?

Applicant: Yes, you're right. That's always a lot harder to answer.

Interviewer: (Pause)

Applicant: (Somewhat hesitatingly) Well, I suppose in the past I may not always have been as assertive as I might have been, and I guess that held me back a bit at New Novelty Manufacturing Company.

Interviewer: You haven't always been as strong or forceful as you would have liked to be.

Applicant: Perhaps so. I mean, I'm not a desk-pounding type of person, and I don't think that approach would go over very well with today's clerical personnel. But I suppose, if you press me on the point, in the past I could have been a little more assertive in advancing my own career. But I find that you catch more flies with honey than with vinegar and, in general, I must say that I've had no trouble in getting people to work for me in the past several years. And I think that I have become more assertive and aggressive in getting things done than I was earlier in my career. Otherwise, I don't think I have any significant limitations that would pose a problem in my work.

Interviewer: I see, Mr. Nelson. Tell me, what are you looking for in a new job?

Applicant: Essentially, Mr. Henderson, I'm looking for a job with a larger company than my present one. I want a job that offers a somewhat better chance for opportunity than I have with Associated Trucking, which is a relatively small organization. I'd also really like a chance to run my own department—not that I don't have any responsibility where I am now. However, I am the number two man in a relatively small organization and most of the decisions are really made by my boss, the office manager. The employment agency indicated that with Universal Life Insurance Company I would have more room to grow and perhaps a chance to run my own department. Is that correct?

Interviewer: Yes, I think that's quite possible. Perhaps this might be a good time for me to give you some information about our company and the job that we have open.

Applicant: Yes, I would be most interested.

Interviewer: Well, as I'm sure you know, Mr. Nelson, Universal is one of the largest life insurance companies in the world, and we have an opening in one of our policy records departments for an office supervisor. Actually, we have several policy records departments throughout the organization and, to some extent, there is a high degree of standardization among them all. There is a procedure that must be followed but, in general, you would be responsible for approximately twelve to fourteen clerical people who prepare, check, and assemble a variety of life, health, and accident insurance policy records. I guess the work is quite similar to what you're doing now and have done before at the department store. Your job would be to assign and distribute work to the people, make sure that the assignments are properly handled, and take care of any problems that might come up during the day. You would be reporting to an office manager and, as is the case with your present job, you would have some say in who gets hired, promoted, and possibly fired from time to time, and you would certainly have the opportunity to recommend salary increases for your people. As you have indicated, you would pretty much be running your own department and its operation. How does that sound to you?

Applicant: (Enthusiastically) It sounds extremely interesting, Mr. Henderson, just what I have been looking for. May I ask what salary you are planning to offer?

Interviewer: Certainly. This job will pay $15,000 per

	year, and I understand from the agency that that is your desired starting salary?
Applicant:	Why yes, it is. You see I am currently earning $13,500 plus a small bonus at the end of the year, and I expect that before too long I will probably be raised if I stay with my present company. So I felt that $15,000 would be an appropriate starting salary.
Interviewer:	I don't see any problem as far as your salary expectations are concerned. Mr. Nelson, do you have any questions that you would like to ask of me?
Applicant:	Well, as you can see, Mr. Henderson, I've had no background in the insurance field whatsoever. Would that be a serious handicap?
Interviewer:	No, by no means. We have a Training Department and you would receive thorough training from our company to orient you to the insurance industry. You have had a good deal of office supervisory experience, of course, and that is the most important consideration. We feel that whatever you need to learn about the insurance business, we will be able to teach you. Do you have any other questions at this time?
Applicant:	Could you comment on opportunities for advancement here at Universal?
Interviewer:	Yes, of course. Wherever possible, we try to promote from within, and being one of the world's largest insurance companies, we obviously have numerous opportunities for personal growth and development. I cannot make any promises, but certainly, if you prove yourself, there is no reason you should not be able to move up.
Applicant:	How about your policy on salary increases?

Interviewer: OK. As far as salary review is concerned, Mr. Nelson, in general you are reviewed on the basis of your work performance on your anniversary date each year. That doesn't automatically guarantee you a salary increase. But we do have a formal appraisal and career review plan, and you and your superior would review your progress very thoroughly once each year. Are there any other questions I can answer for you at this time?

Applicant: Well, I can't think of any for the time being, Mr. Henderson, although I'm sure I will have some more later on. May I ask if my background is what you are looking for?

Interviewer: Yes, I think you have the type of qualifications that we are seeking, Mr. Nelson. I must tell you that we are still interviewing other candidates. However, I can say that we are interested in your background and that we would like to very seriously consider you for this position.

Applicant: I am delighted to hear that, Mr. Henderson. Can you tell me what the next step will be?

Interviewer: Yes, of course. I'm still scheduled to have interviews with several more applicants. But let us see, this is Tuesday. Let us say that you will be hearing from us no later than the end of next week, one way or another, Mr. Nelson. I have your phone number, both at the office and at home, and your mailing address. So, you will hear from us within the next ten days or so.

Applicant: (A bit anxiously) May I ask what my chances are, Mr. Henderson?

Interviewer: Well, as I said, your background looks quite interesting and promising, Mr. Nelson. But, as I also indicated, we still have other

	people to see. I really can't say anything beyond that.
Applicant:	Well, may I say that I'm very much interested in the opportunity with your company, and I do hope that you will consider me.
Interviewer:	You can be certain of that, Mr. Nelson.
Applicant:	Just one more thing.
Interviewer:	What is that?
Applicant:	You're not going to call my present company, are you?
Interviewer:	No, certainly not at this point. However, should an offer of employment be made to you, it will be subject to a satisfactory reference check from your present company. Do you anticipate any difficulty in that area?
Applicant:	No, none whatsoever.
Interviewer:	Well, Mr. Nelson, I enjoyed meeting you and want to thank you for your time. We'll get back to you next week.
Applicant:	Thank you, Mr. Henderson, and goodbye.

Now that you have had the opportunity to read the verbatim transcripts of the two reference checks and the Structured Selection Interview, complete the Interviewer Rating Form (Figure 12) on basic abilities, personal characteristics, and character traits carefully. Particular attention should be paid to the two special sections in Figure 12 calling for the applicant's strong points and weak points for this position, to the overall rating, and, finally, to the decision on whether or not to recommend Mr. Nelson for employment as an office supervisor with Universal Life Insurance Company.

Following Figure 12 you will find my appraisal to compare with your conclusions.

Figure 12. Interviewer rating form on Harry C. Nelson.

HARRY C. NELSON

Applicant's Name _____ Date _____ 19 ___

Position ___OFFICE SUPERVISOR___ Department ___POLICY RECORDS DEPARTMENT___

QUALIFICATIONS

(Check and rate only those that apply to position in question)

	Superior	Very Good	Good	Fair	Poor	Comments

BASIC ABILITIES

- ☐ Intelligence & Mental Alertness
- ☐ Job Knowledge & Skills
- ☐ Education
- ☐ Experience
- ☐ Organizational Skills
- ☐ Communication Skills
- ☐ Energy Level

PERSONAL CHARACTERISTICS

- ☐ Inter-Personal Skills (poise & bearing)
- ☐ Manner & Attitude
- ☐ Inter-Personal Assertiveness
- ☐ Initiative, Drive & Resourcefulness
- ☐ Maturity
- ☐ Motivation & Ambition

CHARACTER TRAITS

- ☐ Stability
- ☐ Industry
- ☐ Perseverance
- ☐ Ability to Get Along With Others
- ☐ Confidence & Self Reliance
- ☐ Leadership

List applicant's strong points for this position

List applicant's weak points for this position

OVERALL RATING

| For This Position | 1 Outstanding | 2 Very Good | 3 Average | 4 Fair | 5 Unsatisfactory |

| Potential for Advancement | 1 Outstanding | 2 Very Good | 3 Average | 4 Fair | 5 Unsatisfactory |

Recommendation to Employ   ☐ Yes   ☐ No   Rated By _____

MY APPRAISAL OF HARRY C. NELSON

Harry C. Nelson is an acceptable, but not outstanding, candidate for this position. He has had a satisfactory, but by no means spectacular, employment record. He is pretty much an average, run-of-the-mill applicant who, in the absence of anyone better, may be employed. As was brought out in the interview, after graduation from college, Mr. Nelson went to work briefly with the Universal Finance Company.

In February of 1968, Mr. Nelson joined the New Novelty Manufacturing Company, but this job soon turned out to be little short of a complete fiasco. He was hired as a production control man and his job was to expedite orders through the plant. However, no matter how hard he worked or how much he tried, he could not satisfy his superior, Mr. T. Brown, the production manager. Mr. Brown was a difficult man to work for—very nervous and erratic and always harassing, pressuring, and abusing people. Mr. Nelson realized before too long that he had made a big mistake in accepting this job and came to the conclusion that he was not suited to a production and manufacturing environment. However, before he had a chance to find another job, Mr. Brown beat him to the punch and fired him. Clearly, although he indicated on the application that he left the New Novelty Manufacturing Company because of a "personality clash" with his superior, this was not the case.

After his discharge from the New Novelty Manufacturing Company, Mr. Nelson was out of work for a period of about four months, during which time he did not have a great deal of success in locating a suitable job. Finally, he found employment with Harris Department Store in Allentown, Pennsylvania, which required relocation to that part of the country. As came out during the interview, Mr. Nelson was substantially successful in improving his department's operations. His superior expressed his appreciation for what Mr. Nelson had done by giving him a $1,000 raise after only six months of employment.

For some time now, Mr. Nelson has been the assistant office manager for Associated Trucking. He has generally done a satisfactory job. Indicative of this fact is that his initial $9,000 salary has reached the $13,500 level. However, more recently Mr. Nelson began to realize that being the number two man under a superior who is only a few years older than he is limits his opportunity for growth. Thus, he made up his mind to look for a better job.

All in all, while he is a *satisfactory* candidate for an office supervisory position, Mr. Nelson is certainly *not outstanding*. So long as he works under moderately close supervision and direction and is handling a fairly structured and clearly defined assignment, he may be expected to do a good job. However, he is not particularly creative, imaginative, or innovative; he does not show that much drive or initiative; and when one gets down to basics, he does not have all that much potential for growth and advancement. Although Mr. Nelson may be expected to perform reasonably well directing the activities of about a dozen clerical employees performing fairly standardized, routine, and repetitive functions, it is unlikely that he will ever advance beyond this level.

All in all, however, while he may not be a superior candidate, there is no reason Mr. Nelson should not be considered for the position. Consequently, my overall rating for Harry C. Nelson is "3" (average qualifications) for this position but only "4" (fair qualifications) for potential for advancement. My final recommendation, in the absence of a superior candidate, is to employ him.

A concluding comment

THROUGHOUT THIS BOOK, I have stressed the many advantages that can be derived from following the Sequential Selection System, a staffing technique intended to make it possible to recruit and select the most competent job applicants with a minimum of wasted time and effort. The system is based on following each of the six sequential steps in the system in order as follows:

Step 1: Determining accurate and realistic staffing specifications.
Step 2: Effective applicant recruiting.
Step 3: Initial applicant screening.
Step 4: Checking the applicant's employment references.
Step 5: Conducting the Structured Selection Interview.
Step 6: Making a final evaluation of the applicant.

The Sequential Selection System has been used for many years with excellent results and has enabled numerous companies to improve the quality and caliber of the employees brought into their organizations markedly. I am convinced that if you use the system proposed in this book, you will be pleased with the results.

One final word, however, may be in order. I do not wish to imply that if you follow the Sequential Selection System, each and every person hired will turn out to be a truly successful and productive employee. Nor will you always be right when you reject someone for employment. Invariably, some applicants will be hired who will fail on the job, while others who should have been employed will erroneously be rejected.

In the final analysis, you should never lose sight of the fact that there is a statistical aspect to the personnel selection process. The personnel professional will never have a perfect batting average, nor would perfection be a realistic expectation. The important thing to bear in mind is how often you are correct in your total evaluation of the applicant's qualifications and ultimately in your final selection decision. It is hoped that some of the suggestions offered here will help you to improve the caliber of the personnel you hire.

appendix A

Tested questions for the structured selection interview

I Work Experience

1. How did you originally get your job with the XYZ Company?
2. Will you describe your present responsibilities and duties?
3. Perhaps you could describe how you spend a typical day?
4. What were some of the things you particularly enjoyed when you were working for the ABC Corporation?
5. What did you enjoy less?
6. What do you consider to have been your major accomplishments at the ABC Company?
7. What were some of the setbacks and disappointments you experienced, or things that turned out less well? Tell me about them.
8. Tell me about the personal progress you made during your association with the XYZ Company.
9. Looking back at the time spent with the ABC Cor-

poration, what do you feel you have gained from your association with the company?

10. In what way has your job changed since you originally joined the company?

11. What were your reasons for leaving the XYZ Company?

12. How would you describe your present (past) superior? What do you consider to have been his major strengths and limitations?

13. In the past, for what things have your superiors complimented you? For what have they criticized you?

14. How do you think your present (past) superior would describe you?

15. What were some of the things about your job that you found more difficult to do?

16. What were some of the problems you encountered on your job and how did you solve these problems?

17. What were some of the things about which you and your superior disagreed?

18. In what way has your present job prepared you for greater responsibilities?

19. What is your impression of your present (former) company?

20. Tell me something about your military experience.

21. How long have you been looking for another position? What type of position are you seeking?

22. As you see it, what would be some advantages to you of joining our company?

23. In what way does the job with our company meet your career goals and objectives?

24. If you joined our organization, where do you think you could make your best contribution? Why?

25. Looking into the future, what changes and developments do you anticipate in your particular field?

26. If you joined our company, what development do you feel you would need to make your best contribution?

II Education

1. Why did you choose the particular college you attended?
2. What determined your choice of major?
3. How would you describe your academic achievement?
4. How did you decide to become an (accountant) (engineer), etc.?
5. In what types of extracurricular activities did you participate?
6. How did you spend your summers while in college (high school)?
7. Did you hold any class or club offices? Which ones?
8. What were your vocational plans at the time of college (high school) graduation?
9. Have you had any additional training or education since graduating from college?
10. How do you think college contributed to your overall development?

III Personal Factors

1. In general, how would you describe yourself?
2. What do you regard to be your outstanding qualities?
3. What do you regard to be some of your shortcomings and developmental needs?
4. In which areas do you feel you would like to develop yourself?
5. What traits or qualities do you most admire in someone who is your immediate superior?
6. What has contributed to your career success up to the present time?

7. What disappointments, setbacks, or failures have you had in your life?
8. How might you further your own business career?
9. What are your long-range goals and objectives?
10. What kinds of situations or circumstances make you feel tense or nervous?
11. How would you describe your health?
12. Have you had any major accidents, illnesses, or operations? Tell me about them.
13. What were some of the major problems or decisions that you have had to make up to the present time?
14. If you had it to do all over again, what changes would you make in your life and career?
15. In considering joining a company, what are some of the factors that you take into account?
16. What are some of the things in a job that are important to you?
17. What would you want in your next job that you are not getting now?
18. What kind of position would you like to hold in five years? In ten years?
19. What are your present salary expectations? How have you arrived at this figure?
20. What are your current recreational and leisure-time interests?
21. Do you presently belong to any social, civic, or professional clubs or organizations? Which ones? Why did you join them?
22. Do you hold office in any of these? Which office?
23. How do you spend your vacations?
24. If you had more time, are there any activities in which you would like to participate? Which ones? Why?

Finally, be sure to ask this question: Are there any additional aspects of your qualifications that we have not covered that would be relevant to the position we are discussing?

appendix B

Sample psychological evaluation of Peter Sanford for Universal Chemical Corporation

As the result of a clinical interview, supplemented by appropriate intelligence and psychological tests, we are pleased to submit to you in confidence our professional evaluation of the qualifications of Mr. Peter Sanford for the position of assistant to the president of your company, the Universal Chemical Corporation.

Recommendation

Mr. Sanford is not considered particularly promising as a candidate for the position in question. He is given an overall rating of "3" on a scale on which "1" represents outstanding qualifications, "2" is above average, "3" is marginal, and "4" is poor. Therefore Mr. Sanford is not recommended for employment.

Although this is an actual evaluation, the names have been changed.

Summary

Despite the fact that Mr. Sanford is truly brilliant and has a great intellectual capacity and could no doubt make a most useful contribution to certain organizations, we do not think he would ever really satisfy your expectations in the position of assistant to the president.

Fundamentally, the problem is that the "fit" between Mr. Sanford's personality and that of your company is not particularly good. Despite his impressive intellectual capacity, Mr. Sanford is not mentally facile. He is a relatively slow, ponderous, and roundabout thinker. Neither his verbal presentations nor his negotiating skills are incisive or persuasive.

Moreover, we do not see Mr. Sanford as a particularly *action-oriented* or *decisive* individual. And while he may regard himself as a potentially successful line operating executive, we, for our part, are more inclined to think that a permanent *staff* assignment where the demands and pressures inherent in the position are not excessive would be much more suited to Mr. Sanford's personality and temperament.

Lastly, to some extent, Mr. Sanford does not impress us as possessing that much business maturity nor, in our judgment, has his past work experience been distinctive. Recognizing your company's demanding expectations—especially with regard to the position in question—we do not feel that, at the age of 34, Mr. Sanford can show particularly outstanding accomplishments.

In short, in our opinion, Mr. Sanford's qualifications do not come close enough to Universal's traditionally high standards. We suggest that you pass him by in favor of an appreciably more promising candidate.

Personal Background

Born and brought up amid comfortable and rather privileged circumstances in northeastern England, the son of the successful owner of a medium-size retail shoe chain, Mr. Sanford is currently 34 years old. He received his secondary education at the well-known Eton School. After graduation, he traveled throughout Europe for six months, and in 1957 he enrolled at Cambridge University. He majored in engineering science and in 1961 received a B.A. degree.

After another six months of travel, Mr. Sanford embarked upon his professional career. Trading on his educational background, he accepted employment with Halliburton & Partners, a London-based firm of consulting engineers, where for the next five and a half years he was involved in the design and construction of various types of water installation facilities.

Toward the spring of 1967, Mr. Sanford began to feel that he needed a greater degree of more generalized business experience. Consequently, he resigned from his engineering position. He traveled for another six months, this time to North Africa and the Mediterranean area, and then decided to emigrate to the United States. In November of 1967, he took on a job similar to the one he had held in England with Harris, McCarthy & Simpson, a firm of consulting engineers located in New York City. The nature of his work with this firm was comparable to that in his previous position. After approximately a year and a half, Mr. Sanford became disenchanted with his job and decided to resign. His salary was then $12,500.

Mr. Sanford went through his by now customary six- to eight-month period of travel, then came to the conclusion that what he wanted to do next was to pursue graduate work in business. Accordingly, he enrolled at the Graduate School of Business at UCLA—primarily because he wanted to live in California—and in June of 1971 he received an M.B.A. degree. He returned to Europe for more travel and, in November of 1971, accepted employment in New York with Texaco. Since that time, he has served as a planning analyst in the Marketing Planning section of Texaco's International Division, where his current salary is $23,500.

Several months ago, Mr. Sanford came to the conclusion that he does not really wish to stay in the oil industry. He feels that the outlook in this business is not particularly promising. Also, he feels that his growth progress at Texaco is apt to be too slow to suit him.

On the personal side, Mr. Sanford is single and rents an apartment in Manhattan. His game plan is to obtain a position that within two or three years would give him enough experience to move into a position of line responsibility in the field of operating management.

Psychological Evaluation

As previously indicated, we are most impressed with Mr. Sanford's level of intelligence. He achieved the highest scores we have ever seen on our firm's various tests measuring mental ability. We are inclined to describe Mr. Sanford's intellectual capacity as virtually unlimited. Accordingly, we think he could undertake just about any assignment given to him and come up with logical and clearly formulated conclusions and recommendations.

However, brilliant as Mr. Sanford may be, we do not think that he would fit the particular bill as assistant to your company's president. In one word, we feel that Mr. Sanford and Universal Chemical would be "mismatched." We do not think Mr. Sanford's personality and basic temperament are suited to your company's pace and tempo.

Fundamentally, as we see him, Mr. Sanford is insufficiently action oriented to give an adequate account of himself within the Universal Chemical environment. Despite his indisputable intellectual ability, Mr. Sanford is not an incisive thinker, nor is he particularly decisive in his actions. Indeed, even though he undeniably is quite personable—poised, urbane, and cosmopolitan in manner —he is also inclined to be professorial and too academic in his approach to business. More specifically, he is not a keen, rapid, or particularly alert thinker. At times, his memory is somewhat faulty, he is often slow to react to a given problem or situation, and he frequently cogitates and hesitates ponderously before arriving at a conclusion.

We also feel that Mr. Sanford's communication skills could profit considerably from sharpening. He is much too expansive verbally, takes a long time to get to the point, and frequently loses his listener along the way. Therefore, we feel that Mr. Sanford would not always be as successful as he should be in persuading or convincing others on a given point, nor do we think that he would be notably effective in overall business negotiations.

In many ways, too, especially recognizing the particular position at stake, we feel that Mr. Sanford lacks sufficient business maturity and prior practical work exposure. To some extent, even though he is already 34, he still has the outlook and perspective of the typical recent graduate of a prestigious, ivy-league business school.

Moreover, we do not feel that Mr. Sanford is quite as settled or directed in his business career as he might be— again noting the assignment for which he is being considered. His track record, in our estimation, is not overly spectacular and is basically limited to seven years of engineering experience supplemented by less than two years as a marketing analyst at Texaco.

Conclusion

In conclusion, then, were he to join your company, we do not think that Mr. Sanford would achieve the kind of results you would expect from him. Intelligent as he may be, we believe that his personality and temperament would prevent him from functioning as effectively as anticipated, either as assistant to your president or as a potential line operating executive, in the foreseeable future. As a result, we feel that a negative recommendation is called for.

appendix C

Selected sources for recruiting minority group and women applicants

ORGANIZATIONAL RESOURCES

1. *The Office of Voluntary Programs, U.S. Equal Employment Opportunity Commission,* 2401 E Street, N.W., Washington, D.C. 20506. The Educational Programs Division has available a detailed listing of "talent banks" and other specialized referral sources throughout the United States. The Talent Search Skills Bank maintains a file of minority and female applicants with professional skills and can refer qualified applicants to prospective employers. In addition, regional offices can furnish information on local referral sources.
2. *Local State Employment Services Offices*
3. *City, County, and State Human Resources Departments and Human Rights Commissions*
4. *Regional Offices of Employment and Training Administration, U.S. Department of Labor*

5. *Americans for Indian Opportunity,* 1820 Jefferson Place, N.W., Washington, D.C. 20036
6. *Bureau of Indian Affairs, Indian Federal Employment Referral Program,* Albuquerque, N.M. 87103
7. *Commonwealth of Puerto Rico, Department of Labor, Migration Division,* 322 West 45th Street, New York, N.Y. 10036
8. *National Alliance of Businessmen,* 1730 K Street, N.W., Washington, D.C. 20006
9. *National Association for the Advancement of Colored People,* 1790 Broadway, New York, N.Y. 10019
10. *National Puerto Rican Forum,* 214 Mercer Street, New York, N.Y. 10012
11. *National Urban League, National Skills Bank,* 477 Madison Avenue, New York, N.Y. 10022
12. *Richard Clarke Associates,* 1270 Avenue of the Americas, New York, N.Y. 10020
13. *Frank Lockett Associates,* 818 Olive Street, Suite 540, St. Louis, Mo. 63101
14. *Fields-Freeman & Associates,* 51 East 42nd Street, New York, N.Y. 10017
15. Local voluntary and privately owned for-profit organizations specializing in the recruitment and placement of minority group and women applicants.

DIRECTORIES AND PROFESSIONAL ROSTERS

1. *Directory for Reaching Minority Groups,* Bureau of Apprenticeship and Training, Office of Information, Employment and Training Administration, U.S. Department of Labor, Washington, D.C. 20210.
2. *Directory of Predominantly Black Colleges and Universities in the U.S.,* National Alliance of Businessmen, 1730 K Street, N.W., Washington, D.C. 20006.
3. *Directory of Minority College Graduates 1971–72.* Prepared by Employment and Training Administration, U.S. Department of Labor. Identifies black, Spanish-surnamed, and other minority graduates of 1971 and 1972 by name, address, degree earned, and major discipline. Superintendent of Documents, Government Printing Office, Washington, D.C. 20402. Computer listings of these graduates by specific educational disci-

plines are available from Office of Equal Employment Opportunity, Office of Assistant Secretary for Employment and Training, U.S. Department of Labor, Washington, D.C. 20210.

4. *Spanish-Speaking Recruitment Sources.* Bulletin of U.S. Civil Service Commission (SSP-75). Comprehensive listing includes junior colleges and colleges with significant SSA enrollment (degrees offered, numbers of SSA students), major media, and organizations and consultants reaching this ethnic group. Superintendent of Documents, Government Printing Office, Washington, D.C. 20402.

5. *Directory of Minority Media.* Prepared by Office of Minority Business Enterprise, U.S. Department of Commerce. Lists newspapers, magazines, and broadcast media that focus on particular racial and ethnic groups, by geographic areas. Also occupational and other statistics of various ethnic and racial groups. Superintendent of Documents, Government Printing Office, Washington, D.C. 20402.

6. *Native American Professional Source Directory.* Lists more than 1,000 American Indian and Eskimo professionals and those close to starting professional careers, with degree, current employment situation, and address. Daniel Honahni, Director, Office of Special Projects, South Western Cooperative Educational Laboratory, 2017 Yale, S.E., Albuquerque, N.M. 87106.

7. *Minority Graduates* (1974). From seventy-five colleges and universities. Includes area of interest and school attended. Ms. Wanda Smith, Student Programs Office, M405 Arkansas Union, University of Arkansas, Fayetteville, Ark. 72701.

8. *Mexican American (Chicano) Handbook of Affirmative Action Programs.* Includes lists of high schools and higher educational institutions with Chicano development programs, names of placement officers, student organizations, numbers of Chicano graduates from selected institutions, and Chicano organizations, predominantly in the Southwest. Personnel Management Association of Aztlan, P.O. Box 4531, Downey, Calif. 90241.

9. *Black Collegian,* 3217 Melpomene Avenue, New Orleans, La. 70125, has published two volumes of résumés of minority college students in accounting, business administration, biology, chemistry, engineering, and mathematics.

10. *Affirmative Recruitment Package.* Lists fifty-seven national and local recruiting sources for women (including minority sources), addresses of state and local Commissions on the Status of Women, and other compilations of women's professional organizations and caucuses. Women's Bureau, U.S. Department of Labor, Washington, D.C. 20210.

11. *Report on Registries.* Lists thirty-six women's professional organizations that maintain registries of employable women in specific fields. Federation of Organizations for Professional Women, 1346 Connecticut Avenue, N.W., Washington, D.C. 20036.

12. *Rosters of Minority and Women Professionals.* Lists approximately seventy rosters of minority and female professionals in the natural and social sciences and engineering. Office of Opportunity in Science, 1515 Massachusetts Ave., N.W., Washington, D.C. 20005.

13. *A Roster of Women and Minority Engineering Students.* Lists 1974 and 1975 graduates from 148 engineering schools. Includes name, field of study, degree level, ethnic group, and personnel office contact. Engineers Joint Council, 345 E. 45th Street, New York, N.Y. 10017.

14. *Directory of Spanish-Surnamed and Native Americans in Science and Engineering.* Includes name, address, academic discipline, and research specialty. Dr. Joseph Martinez, Foundation for Promoting Advanced Studies, 464 Furnace Road, Ontario, N.Y. 14519.

15. *Spanish-Surnamed College Graduates.* A listing of names, addresses, college, and major specialty of graduates with Spanish surnames. Cabinet Committee on Opportunity for the Spanish Speaking, 1707 H Street, N.W., Washington, D.C. 20506.

16. Robert Calvert, Jr., *Equal Employment Opportunity for Minority Group College Graduates: Locating, Recruiting, Employing.* A comprehensive directory listing a variety of useful minority recruiting sources. Garrett Park Press, Garrett Park, Md. 20766.

17. Cecilia H. Foxely, *Locating, Recruiting and Employing Women: An Equal Opportunity Approach.* Lists 300 women's organizations with talent banks and 600 women's placement centers. Garrett Park Press, Garrett Park, Md. 20766.

SELECTED LIST OF
PREDOMINANTLY BLACK COLLEGES

Atlanta University
Atlanta, Ga.

Barber-Scotia College
Concord, N.C.

Benedict College
Columbia, S.C.

Bennett College
Greensboro, N.C.

Bethune Cookman College
Daytona Beach, Fla.

Bishop College
Dallas, Tex.

California State University
Los Angeles, Calif.

Central State University
Wilberforce, Ohio

Claflin College
Orangeburg, S.C.

Clark College
Atlanta, Ga.

Dillard University
New Orleans, La.

Fisk University
Nashville, Tenn.

Florida A & M University
Tallahassee, Fla.

Florida Memorial College
Miami, Fla.

Grambling University
Grambling, La.

Hampton Institute
Hampton, Va.

Howard University
Washington, D.C.

Huston-Tillotson College
Austin, Tex.

Interdenominational
Theological Center
Atlanta, Ga.

Jarvis Christian College
Hawkins, Tex.

Johnson C. Smith University
Charlotte, N.C.

Knoxville College
Knoxville, Tenn.

Lane College
Jackson, Tenn.

LeMoyne-Owen College
Memphis, Tenn.

Livingstone College
Salisbury, N.C.

Miles College
Birmingham, Ala.

Morehouse College
Atlanta, Ga.

Morgan State University
Baltimore, Md.

Morris Brown College
Atlanta, Ga.

Oakwood College
Huntsville, Ala.

Paine College
Augusta, Ga.

Paul Quinn College
Waco, Tex.

Philander Smith College
Little Rock, Ark.

Prairie View A & M University
Prairie View, Tex.

Rust College
Holly Springs, Miss.

St. Augustine's College
Raleigh, N.C.

St. Paul's College
Lawrenceville, Va.

Shaw University
Raleigh, N.C.

Southern University
New Orleans, La.

Spelman College
Atlanta, Ga.

Stillman College
Tuscaloosa, Ala.

Talladega College
Talladega, Ala.

Texas College
Tyler, Tex.

Texas Southern
Houston, Tex.

Tougaloo College
Tougaloo, Miss.

Tuskegee Institute
Tuskegee Institute, Ala.

Virginia Union University
Richmond, Va.

Voorhees College
Denmark, S.C.

Wilberforce University
Wilberforce, Ohio

Wiley College
Marshall, Tex.

Winston Salem State
University
Winston Salem, N.C.

Xavier University
New Orleans, La.

Index